First Look at...
Works 2.0 for the PC

First Look at...
Works 2.0 for the PC

Keiko Pitter

Mitchell McGRAW-HILL
New York St. Louis San Francisco Auckland Bogotá Caracas Hamburg
Lisbon London Madrid Mexico Milan Montreal New Delhi Paris
San Juan São Paulo Singapore Sydney Tokyo Toronto Watsonville

Mitchell **McGRAW-HILL**
Watsonville, CA 95076

First Look at Works 2.0 for the PC

1 2 3 4 5 6 7 8 9 0 DOH DOH 9 0 9 8 7 6 5 4 3 2

ISBN 0-07-050294-3

Sponsoring editor: Roger Howell
Editorial assistant: Laurie Boudreau
Director of production: Jane Somers
Production assistant: Leslie Austin
Project manager: Eve Strock, Bookman Productions
Interior designer: Renee Deprey
Cover designer: Janet Bollow
Cover photo by W. Warren/**West***light*.
Compositor: Winston Sin
Printer and binder: R.R. Donnelley & Sons

Library of Congress Card Catalog No. 91-066891

Contents

Preface

First Look at Works 2.0 for the PC is a step-by-step, hands-on tutorial covering the fundamentals of Microsoft Works for the PC. You can use this book as a self-paced guide, in a lecture class, or as a supplemental text in a variety of classes.

First Look at Works 2.0 for the PC will quickly get you "up to speed" with the program's most useful features. Complete with a comprehensive command summary at the end of the book, *First Look at Works 2.0 for the PC* makes reference quick and easy.

ORGANIZATION

Each lesson contains the following features:

- A list of objectives followed by an overview of the lesson
- A hands-on tutorial that guides students through specific functions and commands
- Note sections that appear throughout the lesson, alerting you to common program pitfalls
- A summary of commands that includes the page number where each command was first introduced
- A self-test that reinforces learning

As you work through *First Look at Works 2.0 for the PC*, you will create files that are used in later lessons. For this reason, it is suggested that you use your own data disk for file storage and retrieval.

FIRST LOOK AT... SERIES

This book is part of the First Look at... series, which consists of titles designed to cover the most popular commercial software packages.

The purpose of each book in this series is to provide an inexpensive, quick, and complete learning tool that you can use for ready reference after you've completed the tutorial. At the end of each book, a comprehensive summary of commands, arranged alphabetically, makes reference easy. It is assumed that you have access to the complete software package and all its features.

In a minimum number of pages, each book covers the most commonly used features of a particular program—enough to equip students with fundamental proficiency in a short time.

ACKNOWLEDGMENTS

I appreciate the efforts of the staff at Mitchell/McGraw-Hill, especially Roger Howell and Laurie Boudreau, who worked tirelessly on this project. Richard Reif, Carl Albert State College, and Sonya Lamle, Okene High School, reviewed the text and offered excellent suggestions.

I thank Richard Pitter for his help, and those educators from across the country who gave me ideas on ways to improve my books. These people were in my classes at the National Computers Educators' Institute at James Madison University in the summer of 1988, Central Oklahoma University in the summer of 1989, and Western Washington University in the summer of 1990. Many of their names appear in exercises in this book.

I extend special thanks to my son, Greg, and my daughter, Jackie, who have learned much about patience and understanding when their mother is working on yet another book.

Keiko Pitter
Salem, Oregon

LESSON ONE

Getting Acquainted with Microsoft Works

OBJECTIVES

In this lesson you will learn how to:

- Use Microsoft Works.
- Start Works.
- Issue mouse and keyboard commands.
- Create a new file.
- Understand the common features of Works.
- Open, close, and save files.
- Print files.
- Get on-screen help.
- Exit Works.

USING MICROSOFT WORKS

Computerized processing of information in Microsoft Works is similar to processing information by hand. Suppose you are a clerk who processes accounts and prepares late notices. You pull out the folders of late accounts and your company's policy on late-payment penalties. With a calculator, pencil, typewriter, and some blank sheets of paper at hand, you set to work. For each account, you do some calculations, type a late notice, and record some information on the account sheet.

If you use Microsoft Works, you can keep customer accounts in a spreadsheet file, late-payment policy data in a database file, and late-payment notices in a word processor file. You can use the spreadsheet to search for and update late accounts and the word processor to edit the late-payment document. Thus, you can generate a personalized notice for each late account. The computer performs the processes that would otherwise be done by hand.

Microsoft Works is an integrated software package, containing tools for word processing, spreadsheet, database, and communications. Spreadsheet charts and database reports can be transferred into word processing documents. The documents you use and edit are called **files** and are stored on disk and retrieved into your computer when you work with them. The main memory of the computer functions a lot like your desktop. You can have several files open simultaneously, you can easily flip from one file to another, and you can transfer data between different files, even if they are in different applications.

A document in memory is an **open file** since it is a file in use. Up to eight files may be open at a time, but only one, called the **active file,** is displayed on the screen. You can easily make another file the active file. While you are working on a document, you can **save** the information to a disk file as a backup measure, and when you have finished using the document, you **close** the file.

STARTING MICROSOFT WORKS

This lesson introduces the basic commands common to all application tools in Microsoft Works. You will have a chance to briefly practice each of these commands. Those commands, such as printing, that have more involved options will be explained later. The commands covered here are the ones you will use each time you use Works. Try to familiarize yourself with them. If you forget a command, you can refer back to this lesson.

To use a computer, the computer must be turned on and the software must be executed. The steps you use depend on whether you have Works installed on a fixed disk (hard disk) or whether you are using Works on a floppy disk (requiring two floppy disk drives).

Starting Works from a Hard Disk

Step A. Turn on your computer.

Step B. When the DOS prompt appears on screen, change the directory to the one that contains WORKS by typing **cd directoryname** and pressing [Enter].

For example, if Works is in the directory WORKS, type **cd works** and press [Enter].

Step C. Type **works** and press [Enter].

The initial screen, shown in Figure 1-1, contains a copyright notice and the File pull-down menu.

Figure 1-1

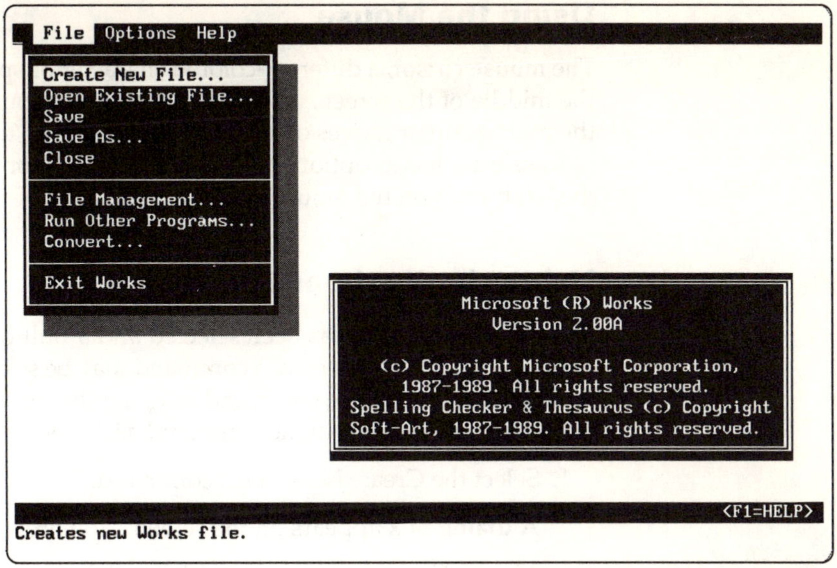

Starting Works from a Floppy Disk

Step A. Turn on your computer.

Step B. When the DOS prompt appears on screen, insert a working copy of the Works Program Disk into drive A.

Step C. Type **Works** and press Enter.

The initial screen, shown in Figure 1-1, contains a copyright notice and the File pull-down menu.

1. Start Microsoft Works using the steps appropriate for your computer system, so that the screen shown in Figure 1-1 appears on your screen.
2. Insert a formatted data disk into drive B.

MOUSE AND KEYBOARD COMMANDS

All the commands in Works can be selected from the keyboard. If your computer has a mouse, you can use it to make command selections. Throughout this book, you will be instructed to select a command or option. You should know how to select commands and options by using the keyboard or the mouse.

Using the Mouse

The **mouse cursor,** a different-colored character or space, is initially located in the middle of the screen. When you move the mouse around on your desk, the mouse cursor moves on the screen in response to the mouse movements.

To select a menu option, move the mouse cursor to that option and press the left button on the mouse.

Using the Keyboard

When a menu option has been selected and a pull-down menu is displayed, as in the initial Works screen, a command may be selected either by typing the highlighted letter of the command or using the up- and down-arrow keys to move the selection bar to the command and then pressing Enter.

1. Select the Create New File... command.

   A **dialog box** appears on the screen. You are to select an application.

   Mouse: You select an option in a dialog box by moving the mouse cursor to that option and pressing the left mouse button.

   Keyboard: You select an option in a dialog box either by typing the highlighted letter of that option or by using the up- and down-arrow keys to move the cursor to that option and pressing Enter.

2. Select <Cancel>.

   The dialog box disappears.

   Next, you will use the menu bar at the top of the screen to display the dialog box again.

   Mouse: A menu option is selected by moving the mouse cursor to that option and pressing the left mouse button. When an option is selected, a pull-down menu opens beneath the option with several commands. If you decide you don't want a selected option, move the mouse cursor to that option on the menu bar and press the left mouse button a second time.

   Keyboard: To select an option from the menu line at the top of the screen, press Alt. Then, either type the highlighted letter of the option you want or use the left- and right-arrow keys to select the option you want and press Enter.

3. Select the File menu option.

   A pull-down menu opens beneath the selected option.

4. Select the Create New File... command.

   The dialog box reappears.

CREATING A NEW FILE

You create new files in Works by using the New command in the File menu and then selecting the application you will use. The filenames have extensions that identify the application: WPS for word processor, WKS for spreadsheet, WDB for database, and WCM for communications.

- Select the <New Word Processor> option.

  The word processor screen appears, as shown in Figure 1-2.

COMMON FEATURES OF WORKS

The top line on the screen is the **menu bar**. You select commands by selecting its options. The bottom line on the screen is the **message line**. It contains a brief message or explanation. Above the message line is the highlighted **status line**. Its information depends on the application.

The screen area between the menu bar and the status line is the work area for the application. The top line of the work area contains the filename, which

Figure 1-2

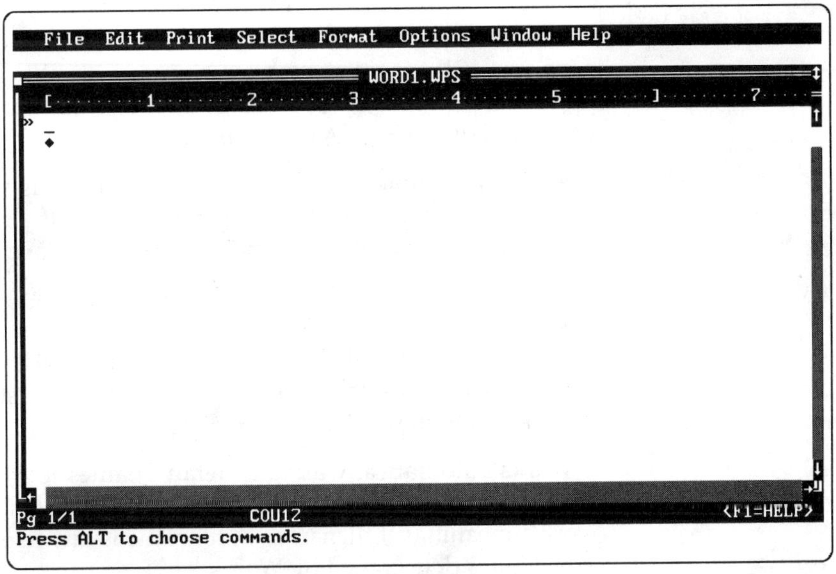

may be WORD1.WPS. (If WORD1.WPS already exists on disk, WORD2.WPS or a similar filename is displayed.)

At the right edge of the work area is a **vertical scroll bar**, which lets you use a mouse to move to any part of the document by moving the mouse cursor to any part of the scroll bar or to the arrow at either end and pressing the left mouse button. At the bottom of the work area, just above the status line, is a **horizontal scroll bar,** which is used similarly. The upper left corner of the work area contains a small square, which is the **close box.** You select that box with the mouse to close the file. The mouse cursor is initially located in the center of the screen.

Some commands have parameters, or options, that need to be specified. When you select such a command (one followed by three dots in the pull-down menu), a dialog box opens in the middle of the screen. You may then need to specify some options, such as the tool or filename. You execute the command by selecting the appropriate command button on the bottom line of the dialog box. If you decide not to execute the command, you select the Cancel option.

Saving, Closing, and Opening Files

Right now, WORD1.WPS is in the main computer memory (RAM). Since you haven't entered anything, it is an empty file. You can enter some information.

1. Type your name and press Enter.

Your document is contained in the main memory of the computer. You can save the file to disk while you are working without leaving the application. When you save a file, you can use either the Save command or the Save As... command.

- When you use the Save command, the file is saved using the filename that appears at the top of the work area. If a file by that name already exists on the disk, the new contents replace the previously existing contents of the file.
- When you use the Save As... command, you are prompted to enter a filename. If a file by that name already exists on disk, another dialog box lets you select whether to replace the existing file or to cancel and return to the dialog box.

Works automatically assigns default names to files. When you save any work for the first time, you should use the Save As... command and give the work a meaningful filename. A filename is one to eight characters long. Its extension is determined by Works.

Figure 1-3

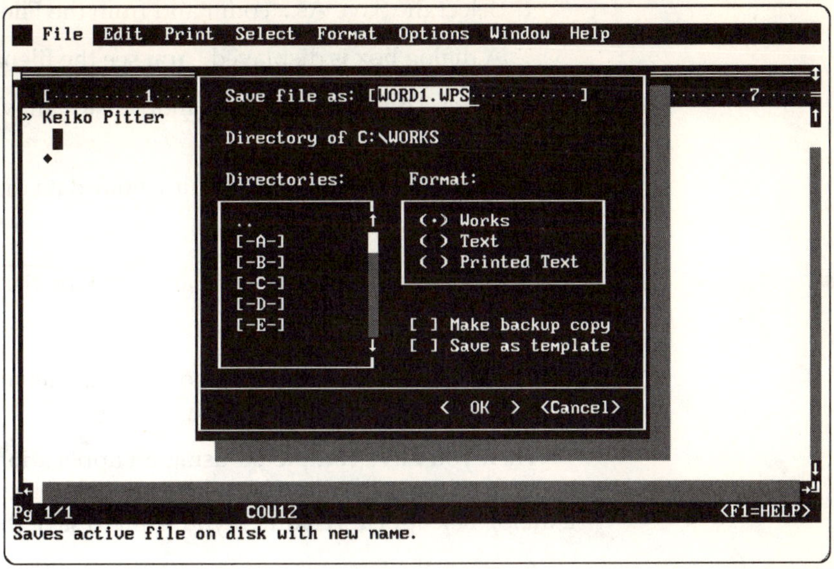

Saving a File Using the Save As... Command

Step A. Select the File menu option and choose the Save As... command. The Save As dialog box, similar to the one shown in Figure 1-3, is displayed.

Step B. In the Directories box, select the drive containing your data disk.

Step C. In the Save file as: box, type a filename.

Step D. Select the <OK> command button at the bottom of the dialog box.

If there exists a file of that name on the disk, Works asks you if you want to replace it. You can replace it or cancel (return to the dialog box).

The file is saved on disk. You can continue to use the file in your application.

Saving a File Using the Save Command

Step A. Select the File menu option and choose the Save command.

The file is saved. You can continue to use the file in your application.

This time, you will save your data in file with a different filename than WORD1.WPS.

1. Select the Save As... command from the File menu.

   A dialog box is displayed. You see the filename WORD1.WPS.

2. Press Tab or use the mouse to move the highlight to the Directories box.

3. Highlight the drive containing your data disk.

4. Press Enter.

   The dialog box indicates that your data disk drive is selected.

5. Enter the filename MYDATA

   The new filename replaced the old filename on the top line of the work area.

When you have completed using an application, you exit from the application by closing the file. If you have modified the file since it was last saved, a dialog box appears asking if you want to save the changes to disk.

6. Select the File menu option and choose the Close command.

   The word processing screen is blanked and Works returns to its initial state.

Applications can use existing files by opening them. Suppose you want to use MYDATA.WPS.

7. Select the Open Existing File... command in the File menu option.

   A dialog box appears. If the appropriate disk drive is selected, MYDATA.WPS appears in the Files box.

8. Make sure the appropriate disk drive is selected.

9. Select MYDATA.WPS in the Files box.

10. Select the <OK> option to open the file.

    The word processing screen appears, displaying the contents of MYDATA.WPS.

Printing a File

When printing the contents of a file, you may need to adjust the format of the output, depending on the application tool you are using. Printing is covered in detail in later lessons. In general, to print a file, you choose the Print... command from the Print menu option, set the options, and execute the command. Right now, you will print the active document.

Figure 1-4

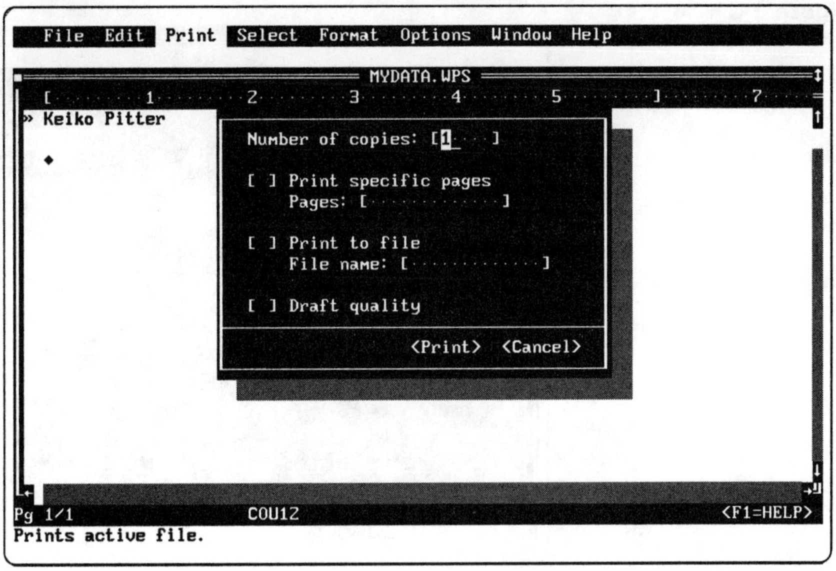

NOTE: It is a good idea to save a file before printing. If anything goes wrong, you can start over by retrieving the file from disk.

1. Make sure that the printer is on and is ready to use.
2. Select the Print... command from the Print menu option.

   A dialog box appears, similar to the one shown in Figure 1-4.
3. Set the various options in the dialog box the same as displayed in Figure 1-4.

   You can set an option by selecting the [ ] box by that option with the mouse or by pressing Tab until the cursor is in that box and then pressing Spacebar.
4. Select the Print command button on the bottom line to begin printing.

   Your document is printed.

   If you need to cancel printing, press Esc.

Getting On-Screen Help

On-screen help is always available in Works. If you need help or information, you can use the help feature. Suppose you want information on how to quit Works.

Figure 1-5

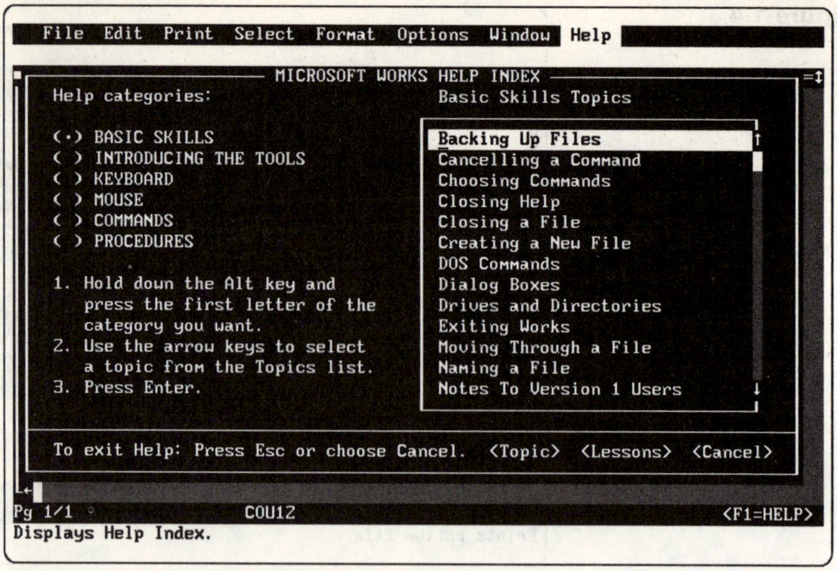

1. Select the Window menu option and choose the Help Index command.

   The screen display looks like Figure 1-5.

   The help feature is organized by topics within broad categories. The topics for the Basic Skills category are displayed in the box. To locate a topic, you may type the first letter of the topic, such as E for exit. If several entries begin with that letter, position the cursor at the correct entry by using the arrow keys.

2. Type **E** for Exit.

   The Exiting Works entry is highlighted.

3. Press Enter.

   Information on the command appears on the screen.

   When you are finished using the help feature, press Esc to return to your previous application.

4. Press Esc.

   You are back in the word processor.

EXITING WORKS

At the end of each Works session, do the following to exit Works:

Step A. Select the Exit command from the File menu option to exit Works and return to DOS.

Step B. For each open file you modified since creating or last saving, a dialog box appears asking if you want to save the changes. Respond accordingly.

Step C. At the DOS prompt, turn off your computer, monitor, and printer.

Step D. Remove your data disk from drive B and carefully store it.

Step E. If you started Works from a floppy disk, remove and store the Microsoft Works program disk.

Exit Works following the above step.

■ *SUMMARY OF COMMANDS*

Topic or Feature	*Command or Reference*	*Menu*	*Page*
Saving a file with new name	Save As...	File	6
Saving a file (same name)	Save	File	7
Printing a file	Print...	Print	8
Closing a file (exit application)	Close	File	8
Creating a new file	Create New File...	File	5
Opening an existing file	Open Existing File...	File	8
Getting on-screen help	Help	Help index	9
Quitting Works	Exit	File	10

■ *SELF-TEST*

1. To give a command in Works, you access an option on the ___________.
2. Using the keyboard, you begin giving a command by pressing the ________ key.

3. Using a mouse, you begin giving a command by ________________.

4. To select a command on a pull-down menu, you ________________.

5. When a command has parameters to be specified, a ____________ appears.

6. To save a file with the same filename, you use the ______________ command.

7. To save a file with a different filename, you use the ______________ command.

8. To use an existing file in an application, you use the ______________ command.

9. To exit an application within Works, you use the ________________ command.

10. To get on-screen help, you first access the ____________ menu option.

LESSON TWO

Word Processing: Creating Documents

OBJECTIVES

In this lesson you will learn how to:

- Understand word processing terminology.
- Enter text into a word processing file.
- Save a file on a disk.
- Position the cursor within the text.
- Delete a block of text.
- Move or copy a block of text.
- Insert text in a document.
- Check spelling.
- Replace one text with another.
- Print the text.

STARTING OFF

First, turn on your computer and start the Works program. Insert your data disk into a disk drive.

STARTING THE WORD PROCESSOR

To use the word processor, you either create a new file or open an existing file for word processing. You will create a new file.

1. Select the Create New File... command from the File menu option.
2. Select the <New Word Processor> option in the dialog box.

   The word processor screen is displayed, as was shown in Figure 1-2 in Lesson One.

The menu bar at the top of the screen displays eight options. At the top of the work area, the **ruler line** indicates the relative positions from the left margin. It indicates the left and right margins by displaying [and], respectively. In a new document, tab stops are preset every half inch, but they are not displayed. Tab stops are discussed in the next lesson.

The filename, WORD1.WPS, is displayed on the top line of the work area. The vertical scroll bar is at the right edge of the work area, and the horizontal scroll bar is at the bottom of the work area. Beneath the work area, the status bar is highlighted. It indicates that you are in page 1 of 1 in the document. The font depends on your printer; in Figure 1-2 the word COU12 stands for 12-point Courier (10 characters per inch). At the right, the screen indicates that the F1 function key is a shortcut for getting on-screen help. At the bottom, the message line displays a message.

On the line beneath the ruler line, the blinking underscore, or **cursor**, shows where your entries are made. To the left of the cursor is the symbol », the beginning-of-page marker. Beneath the cursor is the symbol ♦, the end-of-file marker.

ENTERING TEXT

To enter text, you use your keyboard like a typewriter, except you do not enter a carriage return when you fill up a line. Just keep on typing, because when the cursor gets beyond the right margin, it reappears at the left margin, one line down. If a word extends beyond the right margin, it is moved intact to the next line. When you finish a paragraph, press Enter. The Enter key breaks the line and moves the cursor to the left margin of the next line. You press Enter twice to insert a blank line between paragraphs.

When your text fills up the work area, the text will **scroll up**—that is, a new line will appear at the bottom of the work area, and the uppermost line will disappear from the screen.

Moving the Cursor

You can move the cursor to a new position in the text by using either the mouse or the keyboard.

Mouse: To relocate the cursor on the screen, move the mouse cursor to the new position and press the left mouse button. To scroll the text, move the mouse cursor to an arrow symbol at either end of a scroll bar and press the left mouse button.

Keyboard: The arrow keys move the cursor one position in the indicated direction. [Home] and [End] move the cursor to the beginning and end, respectively, of the line. [Pg Up] moves the cursor one screen up or to the beginning of the text. [Pg Dn] works similarly, in the opposite direction.

Correcting Errors

If you make a typing error, you can delete unwanted characters by moving the cursor to the character and pressing [Delete] or by moving the cursor to the right of the character and pressing [Backspace].

Uppercase Letters

To type uppercase letters, hold down [Shift] while you type the character, just as you would on a typewriter. If you want to type a series of capital letters, press [Caps Lock] once, just as you would do with the shift-lock key on a typewriter. To return to lowercase, press [Caps Lock] again. To enter nonalphabetic shifted characters, such as $ or), hold [Shift] down regardless of the [Caps Lock] position.

Now enter the following text:

> **Records of transactions, contracts, and inventories form the basis that allows business to be conducted in an orderly manner. Scribes have been used through the ages to produce copies of business contracts. Inventions which have lowered the cost or increased the speed for an individual to write a document have resulted in increased business productivity. These inventions include paper, ball point pens, and typewriter. The personal computer did not become a success until it became useful for business. Today, word processing is the most common business use of personal computers.**

SAVING YOUR WORK

You must save your text on a disk if you plan to use it during another session. Lesson One described saving files to disk. You will save your text as MYFILE on your data disk.

1. Make sure your data disk is in a disk drive.
2. Select the Save As... command from the File menu.

   A dialog box appears, with the original filename, WORD1.WPS, selected.

3. If necessary, select the drive with your data disk and select the <OK> button.
4. Type **MYFILE** in the filename box.
5. Press [Enter].

   Works saves the document on disk.

   You return to the word processor.

CHANGING TEXT

You may make changes anywhere in the text by deleting unwanted characters and typing the new text. To delete unwanted characters:

- Place the cursor to the immediate *right* of characters you wish to delete and press [Backspace] to erase unwanted characters.

  or

- Place the cursor *on* the character and press [Delete].

Since [Backspace] and [Delete] delete one character, if you wanted to delete 100 characters, you would have to press [Backspace] 100 times. There is an easier way to delete larger portions of text: You **select** a portion of text and then press [Delete].

1. Place the cursor to the left of the first character of the second sentence—that is, to the left of the character S of "Scribes have. . . ."
2. Select a block of text using either the mouse or the keyboard.

   Mouse: Hold down the mouse button and drag until you've highlighted the text "Scribes have been use through the ages to produce copies of business contract." Then release the button.

   Keyboard: Hold down [Shift] while you use the arrow keys to highlight the text noted above.

   When the sentence is selected, the screen will look similar to Figure 2-1.

3. Press [Delete].

   The selected text disappears.

Figure 2-1

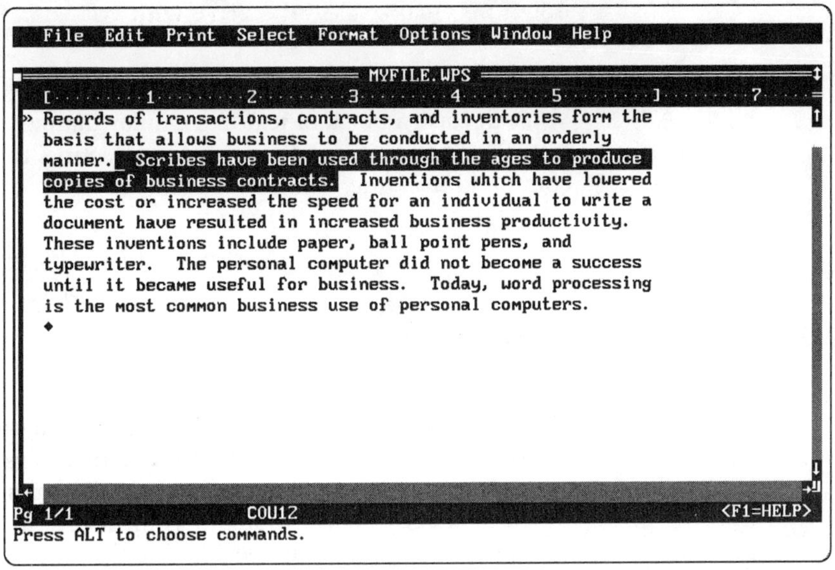

MOVING TEXT

To move a block of text from one location to another, you select the text and then you use the Move command.

1. Place the cursor immediately after the next-to-last sentence—that is, on the blank space following the word "business."
2. Select the sentence "Today word processing is the most common business use of personal computers."
3. Select the Move command from the Edit menu.

   The message at the bottom of the screen prompts you to select the new location and press Enter.
4. Move the cursor to the space just before the fourth sentence—that is, immediately after the word "typewriter."
5. Press Enter.

   The selected text moves to the cursor position.
6. For practice, move that sentence back to its original position.

COPYING TEXT

You can copy a block of text in a similar manner. Copied text is not deleted from the original position. After selecting the text, you use the Copy command from the Edit menu.

INSERTING TEXT

If you need to insert a word in the middle of a sentence or a sentence in the middle of a paragraph, position the cursor where you want to insert the text and start typing. Text to the right of the cursor is pushed across the line and down the page to make room for your insertion. You position the cursor by using the arrow keys or by positioning the mouse cursor and pressing the left button.

1. Position the cursor before the word "Inventions" in the second sentence.
2. Type the following text just as it appears (with errors):

   The earliest writing, cuneiform inscriptoins on on clay tablets, often kept business recrds.

   Your screen should look similar to Figure 2-2.

Figure 2-2

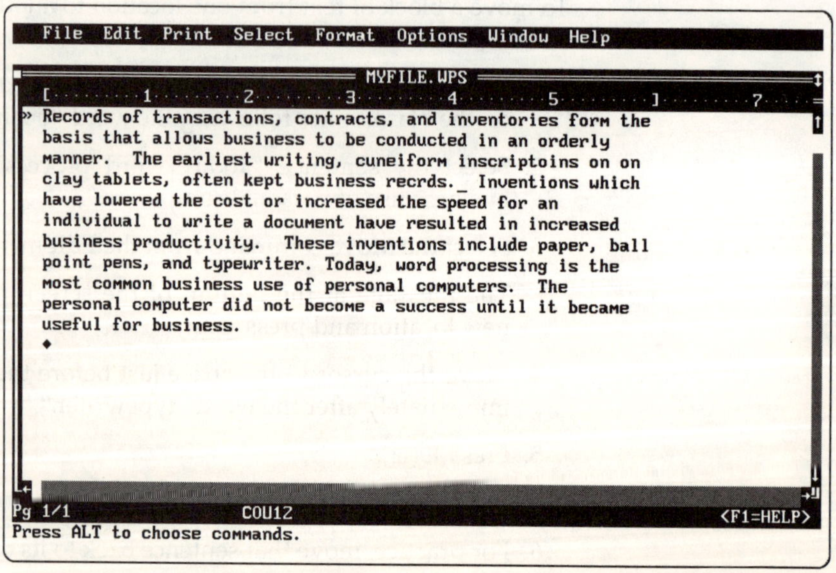

CHECKING SPELLING

You entered a sentence with errors. You will now use a spelling checker. When you use the spelling checker, Works compares each word in the document with a list of correctly spelled words, known as a **dictionary**. The program flags those words that are not in the dictionary, and for each of these words it displays words from the dictionary that you might have wanted.

1. Position the cursor at the beginning of the text.
2. Select the Check Spelling... command from the Options menu.

   The Check Spelling dialog box appears, with "inscriptoins" highlighted. In this case, the spelling checker does not have any suggestions. You need to type "inscriptions" correctly.
3. Type **inscriptions** and press [Enter].

   The repeated word "on on" is highlighted and the dialog box suggests replacement with "on."
4. Press [Enter] to correct the duplicated word.

   The dialog box displays the incorrect word "recrds."
5. Type **records** and press [Enter].

   When the spelling checker is finished, a dialog box is displayed.
6. Select <OK>.

REPLACING TEXT

You can easily replace a word or phrase with different text.

1. Select (highlight) the text "personal computer" in the next-to-last sentence.
2. Select the Typing Replaces Selection command from the Options menu.
3. Type **microcomputer** and press [Enter].

   The highlighted text is deleted and replaced by what you type.
4. For practice, change "microcomputer" back to "personal computer" in the text.

PRINTING TEXT

You will now print the text.

1. Make sure that your printer is turned on and ready to use.
2. Select Print... from the Print menu.

   A dialog box is displayed as shown in Figure 2-3.

Figure 2-3

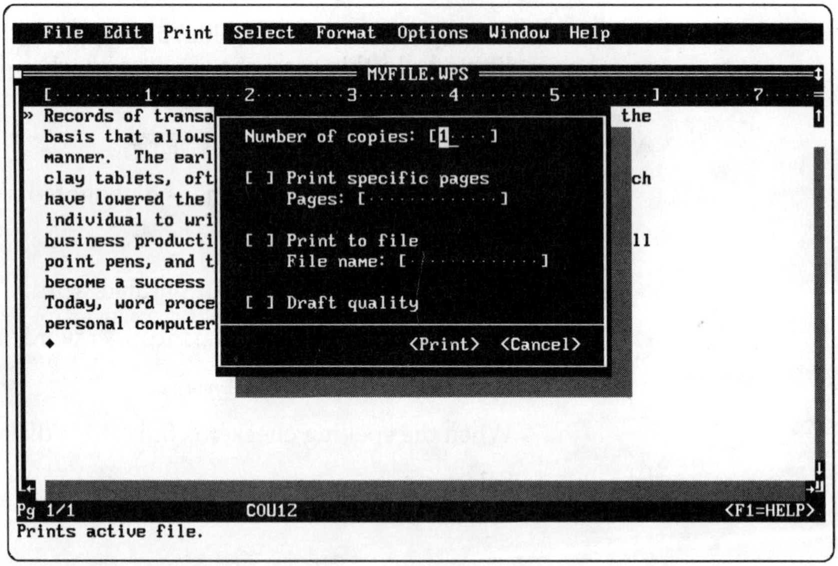

3. If the dialog box on your screen does not have the same options selected as shown in Figure 2-3, change the options to make them the same.
4. Select **Print.**

   Your document is printed.

QUITTING THE SESSION

This is the end of this lesson. To quit properly, follow the instructions given in Lesson One. Save the changes you made to your file.

■ SUMMARY OF COMMANDS

Topic or Feature	*Command or Reference*	*Menu*	*Page*
Selecting text or data	*Mouse:* Hold down button while highlighting text or data. *Keyboard:* Hold down [Shift] while using arrow keys to highlight the text or data.		16
Deleting text	Select the text, then press [Delete]		16
Moving text	Select date to be moved and then Move Position cursor; press [Enter]	Edit	17
Copying text	Select the text and then Copy	Edit	18
Inserting text	Place the cursor where you want text inserted, then type the text		18
Checking spelling	Check Spelling...	Options	19
Replacing text	Select the text to be replaced and then Typing Replaces Selection	Options	19
Printing text	Print...	Print	20

■ SELF-TEST

1. A portion of the text is selected by ____
____.
2. To replace one word with another, you ______________________________.
3. When you ______________ (move/copy) text, it is removed from its original position in the document.
4. Spelling checkers ______________ (can/cannot) detect all spelling errors.
5. Text can be printed by selecting the PRINT... command from the ______________ menu option.

6. To type a ? or (character, you must hold down the ______________ key.
7. The » symbol is the ___________________ marker, and the ♦ symbol is the __________________ marker.
8. To copy text, you use the ______________________ command in the ______________ menu option.
9. When text fills up the screen, some of it ______________ as you enter more text.

LESSON THREE

Word Processing: Formatting Documents

OBJECTIVES

In this lesson you will learn how to:

- Retrieve an existing file from disk (open the file).
- Recognize some of the default format settings.
- Specify page setup and margins.
- Use the Format menu:
  - First-line indentation;
  - Paragraph indentation;
  - Outdenting;
  - Tab stops;
  - Justification;
  - Bold/underline;
  - Line spacing.
- Copy formatting within a document.
- Switch between open files.

STARTING OFF

Start your personal computer and enter the Works program, as described in Lesson One. Insert the data disk you used in Lesson Two into a disk drive. First you will work with the text you saved in the last lesson.

1. Select the Open Existing File... command from the File menu option.
2. If necessary, select the drive that contains your data disk and select the <OK> button.
3. Highlight the file MYFILE.WPS and select the <OK> button.

   The text from the previous lesson is displayed on the screen.

FORMATTING A DOCUMENT

You might have noticed that when you printed the text at the end of the first lesson, it printed the way it was displayed on the screen. Since the screen display format was preset by Works (you were using the default settings), the document may not have been printed the way you wanted.

You can change your document's format. There are two places where the appearance of a document is specified: the Page Setup & Margins... command in the Print menu and the Format menu.

- The Page Setup & Margins... command lets you select the paper size, margin settings, and beginning page number. These specifications affect the entire document.
- The Format menu commands let you specify indentations, tab stops, justification, size, style (underline, bold), appearance (font), and spacing of text. When you set options in the Format menu, some of the settings affect the paragraph that the cursor is in, and others affect characters being entered, until another setting is specified (upon which the new specifications take effect). You can also change the appearance of text already entered by highlighting it and specifying the format desired.

PAGE LAYOUT

First you will specify formatting through the Layout command.

Select the Page Setup & Margins... command from the Print menu.

A dialog box appears, as shown in Figure 3-1.

This dialog box lets you specify paper size, margins, and the beginning page number. These settings affect the appearance of the entire document. To change the settings, you select the appropriate options using the mouse or Tab from the keyboard. By default, the paper selected is 8 1/2 inches wide by 11 inches long.

Margin Settings

The top and bottom margins are initially 1 inch, whereas the left margin is 1.3 inches and the right margin is 1.2 inches. You will now change the left margin to 2 inches.

Figure 3-1

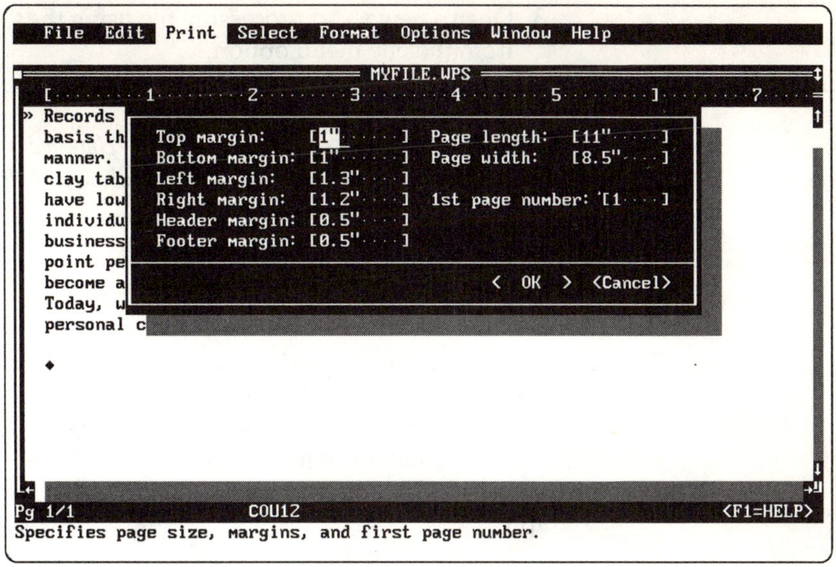

1. Select the left margin box.
2. Type **2**.
3. Press Enter.

   You return to the document.
4. Now change the right margin to 2 inches.

RULER LINE

Just above the work area is the ruler line. On the ruler line, the positions of the printed text are noted, with each tenth position numbered. The left-indent marker ([) is positioned at 0 inches. The right-indent marker (]) is positioned at 4.5 inches. The left-indent marker tells how much the text is to be indented relative to the left margin, which you set in Page Setup & Margins. The right-indent marker tells the line width.

PRACTICE TIME

1. Get a printout of the text.
2. Close MYFILE, saving changes.

3. Open a new word processing file using the Create New File... command from the File menu option.

NOTE: Any Layout settings that were changed for MYFILE are internal to MYFILE. The new file you just created still carries all the default settings.

Line Indentation

Suppose you want to indent the first line of a paragraph by 1/2 inch. You can do this by setting the **first-line indent** to 0.5 inch. The first-line-indent marker (|) is initially at the same position as the left indent marker ([). Once the first-line-indent marker is positioned, Works will indent the first line of each paragraph. All you need to do is press Enter at the end of each paragraph.

1. Select the Indents & Spacing... command from the Format menu option.
2. Select the 1st Line Indent box.
3. Type **0.5** and press Enter.

   The first-line-indent marker is positioned at 0.5 inch on the ruler line, as shown in Figure 3-2.

Figure 3-2

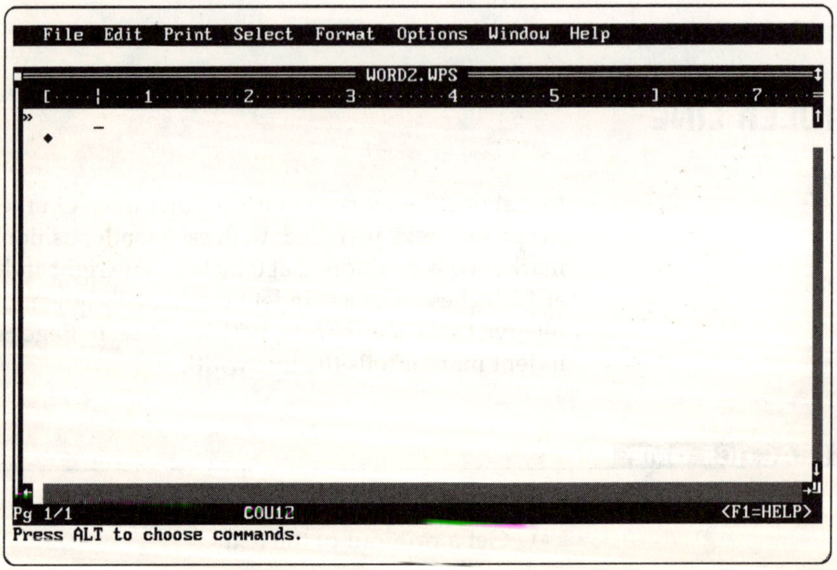

PRACTICE TIME

1. Enter the following text:

   When a computer is instructed to do a job, it handles the task in a very special way. It accepts the information. It stores the information until the information is ready to be used. It processes the information. Then it gives out the processed information.

2. Get a printout of the text.
3. Save this file on your data disk as FILE2.

Paragraph Indentation

Sometimes you need to indent a whole paragraph, such as when you are quoting from a book. To do this, you change the values of the **left** and **right indents** for a while. To indent each line of a paragraph, you change the left indent and set the first-line indent to 0.

1. Place the cursor at the end of the text.
2. Press [Enter] to insert a blank line.
3. Select the Indents & Spacing... command from the Format menu option.
4. Set left indent to 1 inch and first-line indent to 0 inch.
5. Type the following:

   The concept behind word processing is a fascinating one. The type-writer has become archaic, stricken by a single technological blow. The concepts of training and productivity have changed, too. The more productive worker is the one who can insert text changes, make corrections, move blocks of text, and otherwise process text rewrites efficiently.

6. Insert a blank line after the paragraph.

PRACTICE TIME

1. Change the left indent and first-line-indent settings back to their original values so that the text that follows is indented only on the first line.

2. Type the following:

   We no longer train people to type 60-plus words per minute, error free.

3. Save the text using the Save command.
4. Print the text.

Outdenting

You can also **outdent** a paragraph, creating a hanging paragraph. In contrast to indenting the first line of a paragraph, outdenting a paragraph means extending the first line to the left.

1. Place the cursor anywhere within the first paragraph.
2. Select the Indents & Spacing... command from the Format menu option.
3. Change the left indent to 0.5 inch and the first-line indent to – 0.5 inch.

   The first line of the paragraph is outdented.

   Your screen should look similar to Figure 3-3.

Figure 3-3

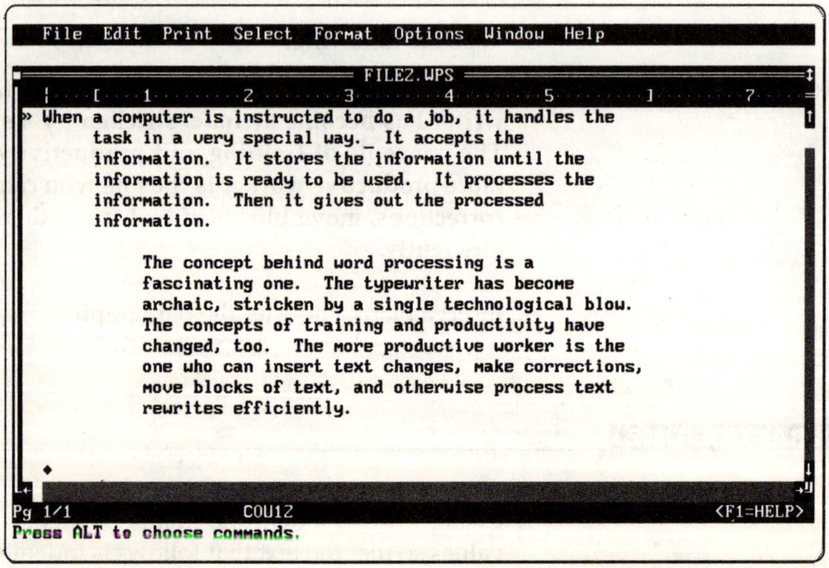

PRACTICE TIME

1. Delete the first paragraph and, in its place, enter the following:

   When a computer is instructed to do a job, it handles the task in a very special way.

2. Press [Enter] twice.
3. Move the left-indent marker to the 1.5-inch position.
4. Set the first-line indent marker to – 0.5 inch.
5. Enter the following. Be sure to press [Tab] after each number.

   1. It accepts the information.

   2. It stores the information until it is ready to be used.

   3. It processes the information.

   4. It gives out the processed information.

   Your screen should look like Figure 3-4.

6. Save the file as FILE3.

Figure 3-4

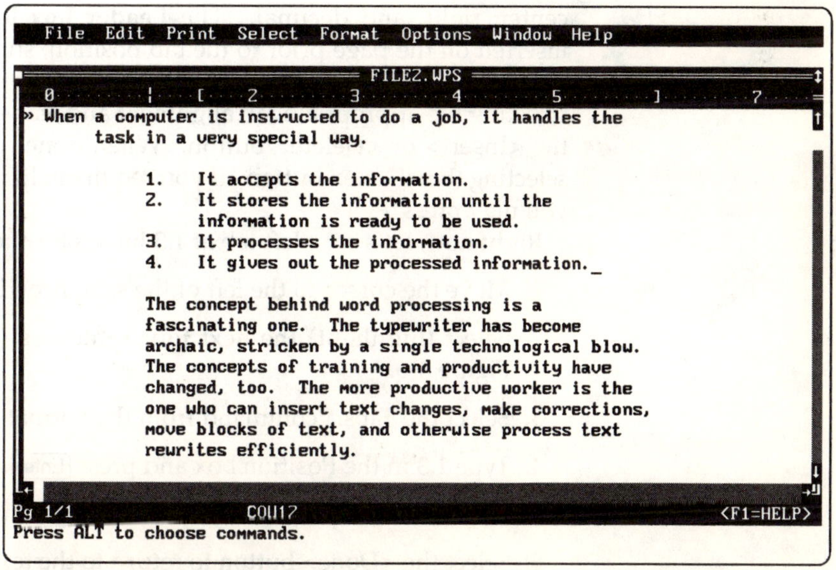

Figure 3-5

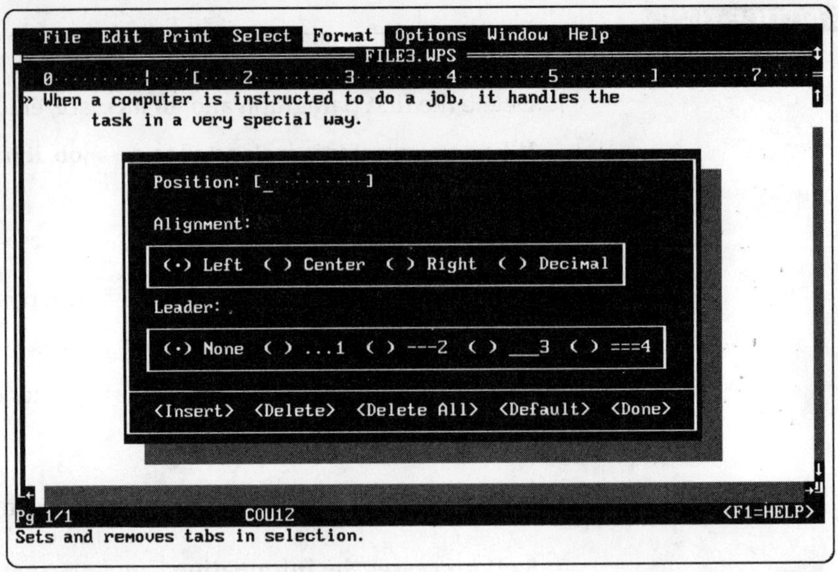

Setting Tabs

By default, tabs are set to every half inch. You can set your own tabs. When you set a tab, all default settings to the left of the new ones are erased. To set a tab, select the Tabs... command from the Format menu option. A dialog box appears, as shown in Figure 3-5.

The **Alignment box** lets you select from four types of tab alignments: left, center, right, and decimal. The **Leader box** lets you specify characters inserted on the page prior to the tab position, such as in a table of contents. You set and clear tab stops by entering the tab position in the **Position box,** selecting the appropriate tab alignment and leader, and then selecting either the <Insert> or <Delete> button. When done, you return to your text by selecting the <Done> button. If you require help while using this dialog box, you may press F1.

Right now, let's set a left tab at 1.3 inches for the outdented paragraphs.

1. Move the cursor to the left of the sentence "1. It accepts. . . ."
2. Select (highlight) the next four sentences (paragraphs), as shown in Figure 3-6.
3. Select the Tabs... command from the Format menu option.
4. Type **1.3** in the Position box and press Enter.

   A left tab is displayed on the ruler line as an L at that position.
5. Select the <Done> button to return to the text.

On the ruler line, the L at 1.3 inches indicates a left tab.

The text in the selected paragraphs adjusts to the tab stops at 1.3 inches.

PRACTICE TIME

1. Set another left tab at 0.8 inch.
2. Move the first line indent marker to – 1.1 inches (relative to the left-indent position for the highlighted paragraphs).
3. Save the file as FILE4.

Figure 3-6

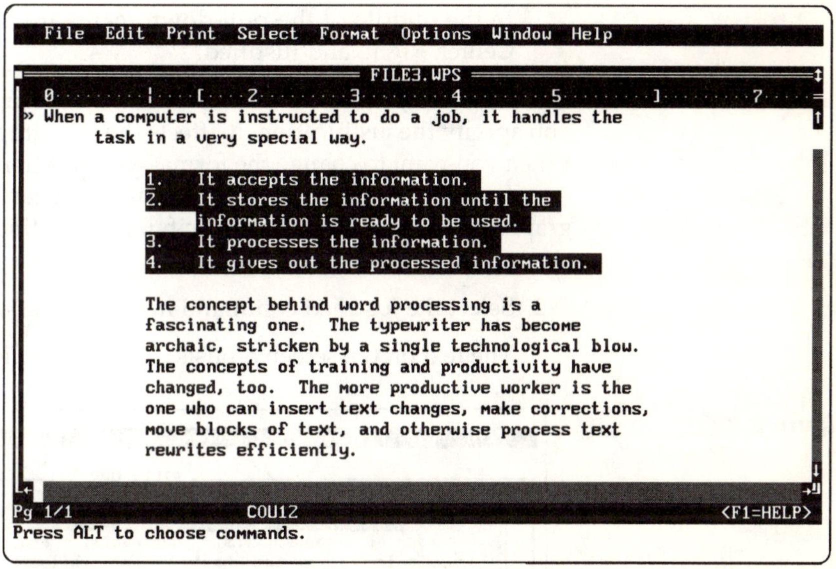

OPENING ANOTHER FILE

You will now use file MYFILE while FILE4 remains in the main memory of the computer.

1. Select the Open Existing File... command in the File menu option.
2. Select MYFILE.

   The text for MYFILE appears on the screen.

MYFILE becomes the active file, but FILE4 remains open in main memory. The top and left edge of the work area indicate that FILE4 is open but not active.

JUSTIFICATION

The default setting for text justification is Left. That means that the left margin is aligned, but not the right margin. The alignment of text can be changed through the Justification option in the Format menu.

1. Select the Format menu.

   In the middle of the pull-down menu are the command options Left, Center, Right, and Justified.

If you select Justified, both the left and right margins will be aligned. When you specify the justification, it affects the paragraph that contains the cursor. When you want to change the format, you position the cursor and change the specification again. You can also change the justification of multiple paragraphs by selecting them and specifying the justification. Right now, you will change the alignment to Justified.

2. Select the Justified command in the Format menu.

   The text on the screen adjusts as shown in Figure 3-7.

Figure 3-7

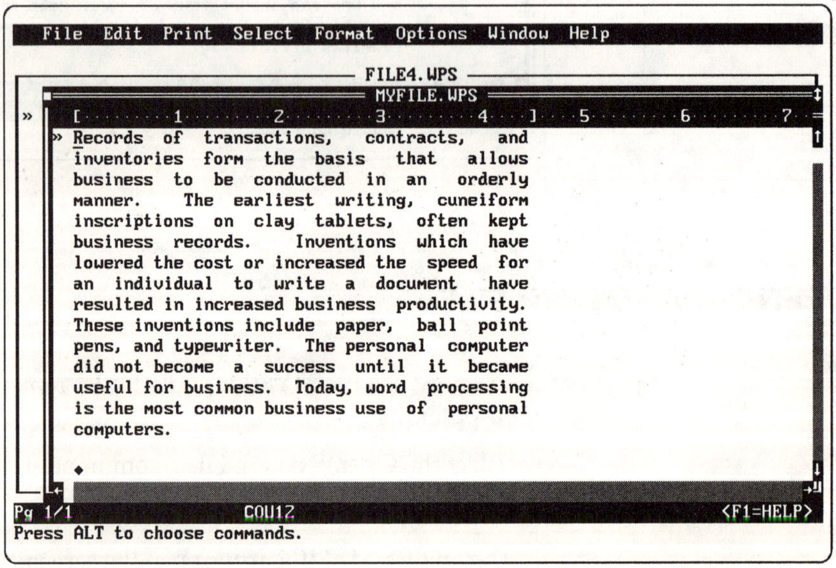

If you want to center text, such as when you enter a title, you position the cursor where you are entering the title, specify center justification, and start typing.

3. Position the cursor at the beginning of the text.
4. Press [Enter] twice to insert two blank lines.
5. Position the cursor on the first line.

PRACTICE TIME

Specify Center justification.

---

6. Type **WORD PROCESSING EXAMPLE.**

   As you type, the characters appear in the middle of the line, centered between the line indent markers.

BOLD/UNDERLINE

Suppose that you want the title to appear in bold characters. You can probably figure out how to do this.

1. Select (highlight) the text containing the title.
2. Select the Bold command from the Format menu.

   The title is now in bold characters.

3. Position the cursor at the end of the text; then press [Enter] to insert a blank line.

If you want characters to appear in boldface as you type, you can enter the specification for bold. Then the characters that follow will be bold until you enter the specification to stop it.

1. Select the Bold command from the Format menu.

   A "B" appears on the status line, indicating that the text at the cursor position is bold.

2. Type the following:

   This text is entered as bold characters.

3. To turn off the bold style, select the Plain text option from the Format menu.

   The "B" disappears from the status line.

4. Now type the following: **The characters are no longer in bold.**

NOTE: To turn the bold style on, you can enter Ctrl-B. *That is, hold down* Ctrl *and press* B.

Underlining text works the same as creating bold text. You can choose underline from the Format menu or enter Ctrl-U. You can experiment on your own with other styles on the menu. They all work the same way.

LINE SPACING

Microsoft Works lets you single- or double-space your document. You can set spacing from the Format menu. Spacing affects the paragraph that contains the cursor. You can also change the spacing of multiple paragraphs by highlighting them and choosing the appropriate spacing.

1. Position the cursor anywhere in the first paragraph.
2. Choose the Double Space command from the Format menu.

   The first paragraph is now double-spaced.

PRACTICE TIME

1. Change the paragraph back to single spacing.
2. Make FILE2 the active file. (Select that file from the Window menu.)
3. Change the paragraph beginning with "The concept behind word processing" to justified and double-spaced.

COPYING FORMAT

When you have specified the format for a paragraph, it is possible to copy the format to another paragraph. Right now, you will copy the format of the first paragraph to the one following the four points. The format includes indentation.

1. Position the cursor anywhere on the first paragraph.
2. Select the Copy Special... command from the Edit menu.
3. Position the cursor anywhere on the paragraph beginning with "The concept behind word processing."
4. Press [Enter].

   A dialog box appears, with two options: Character format or paragraph format.
5. Select Paragraph Format.

   The paragraph formatting is copied.

QUITTING THE SESSION

This is the end of this lesson. To quit properly, follow the instructions given in Lesson One. Save your changes.

■ *SUMMARY OF COMMANDS*

Topic or Feature	*Command or Reference*	*Menu*	*Page*
Setting margins	Page Setup & Margins...	Print	24
Setting paragraph indentations	Indents and Spacing...	Format	27
Setting tab stops	Tabs...	Format	30
Setting justification	Left, Center, Justified	Format	32
Setting character style	Bold, Underline, Plain Text	Format	33
Entering bold text	[Ctrl]-[B]		34
Entering underlined text	[Ctrl]-[U]		34
Setting line spacing	Single Space, Double Space	Format	34
Copying paragraph format	Copy Special...	Edit	34
Opening second file	Open Existing File...	File	31
Switching between open files	Select file	Window	34

■ SELF-TEST

1. To set margins, you use the __________ command from the __________ menu option.
2. The ruler line indicates left and right paragraph indentations by the ____ and ____ characters.
3. The first line indentation of a paragraph is set using the __________ command from the __________ menu option.
4. To outdent a paragraph, the first line indentation is set to __________ (a positive value, a negative value, zero).
5. Tabs are set using the __________ command from the __________ menu option.
6. To switch among open files (to make another file the active file), the __________ menu option is used.
7. A justified paragraph means __________.
8. Underline can be set from the Format menu or by using the __________ keystroke.
9. Single- or double-spacing is set from the __________ menu option.
10. A paragraph format is copied using the __________ command from the __________ menu option.

LESSON FOUR

Word Processing: Editing Documents

OBJECTIVES

In this lesson you will learn how to:

- Move or copy a block of text from one word processing file to another.
- Enter text with right justification.
- Set tabs with left, right, or decimal alignment.
- Find a particular word or combination of words in a text.
- Replace a particular word or combination of words in a text with a specified word or combination of words.
- Make page breaks.
- Control printing of page numbers on the page.

STARTING OFF

Start up your computer and enter the Works program so that the Open dialog box is displayed. Insert your data disk from Lesson Three into a disk drive.
You will start by retrieving MYFILE and FILE2 from the data disk.

PRACTICE TIME

Open files MYFILE and FILE2. Make FILE2 the active file (the one displayed on the screen).

COPYING AND MOVING TEXT

Sometimes you need to take a passage out of one document and include it in another. In Microsoft Works, information can be copied or moved from one document into another word processing document.

You will copy the second paragraph from FILE2 into MYFILE.

1. Select (highlight) the second paragraph.
2. Select the Copy command from the Edit menu.

   The message line reads:

```
Select new location and press ENTER or press ESC to cancel.
```

   The status bar indicates that you are in the COPY mode.

3. Select MYFILE from the Window menu.
4. Move the cursor to the end of the document.
5. Press [Enter] to insert the copied text at the cursor, as shown in Figure 4-1.

Figure 4-1

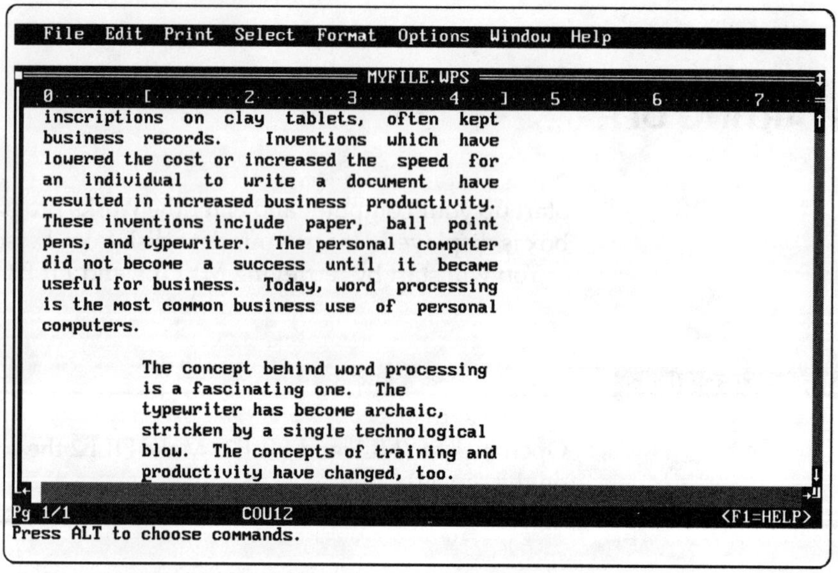

PRACTICE TIME

Copy the first paragraph from MYFILE into FILE2 as its second paragraph.

ENTERING TEXT RIGHT JUSTIFIED

Usually, you want your text aligned at the left. If you want the text to be aligned at the right as well, you want the text **justified.** There are also times when you want the text to be entered **right justified** (aligned with the right margin) without any regard to the left margin, for example, when you are entering the date at the beginning of a letter.

1. Create a new word processing file.
2. Select the Right command from the Format menu.

   The cursor appears at the position of the right indent marker.
3. Type **December 14, 1991,** and press Enter.

   The text is right justified—even with the right margin.

The text will continue to be right justified until you change the alignment.

PRACTICE TIME

1. Enter the following partial letter. You can work around the date that is already entered.

   1728 Forest Road
   Takoma Park, MD 20912
   December 14, 1991

   Mr. Gary Bradshaw
   Computer Parts Shop
   1234 Byte Street
   Golden, CO 80401

   Dear Mr. Bradshaw:

   Please accept my order for the following items:

2. Save the text as LETTER1.

TAB ALIGNMENT

In the letter you started, the next step is to specify the items you want to order, quantity, and price, as shown next:

50	**boxes of diskettes @14.75**	**$737.50**
5	**printer ribbons @11.95**	**59.75**
1	**diskette container @9.95**	**9.95**

You will enter the first column right justified at 1 inch, the second column left justified at 1.5 inches, and the third column aligned with the decimal point at 5 inches. You can set the tabs so that this type of data entry is simple.

1. Make sure that the cursor is at the bottom of the text. There should be at least one blank line after the end of the text.

   You will set tabs at 1, 1.5, and 5 inches. However, you want a right tab at 1 inch, a left tab at 1.5 inches, and a decimal tab at 5 inches.

2. Select the Tabs... command from the Format menu.
3. In the Position box, type **1** (do not press Enter).
4. In the Alignment box, select Right.
5. Select the <Insert> button.

   An R appears on the ruler line at 1.0 inch, indicating a right tab.

6. Similarly, insert a Left tab at 1.5 inches.
7. Finally, insert a Decimal tab at 5.0 inches.
8. Select the <Done> button to exit the Tabs dialog box.

   The ruler line indicates the positions of the left and decimal tabs, as shown in Figure 4-2.

9. Press Tab.

   The cursor jumps to the 1.0-inch position.

10. Type **50**.

    The entry is right justified at the 1-inch position.

11. Press Tab.

    The cursor jumps to the 1.5-inch position.

12. Type **boxes of diskettes @14.75.**

    The entry is left justified at the 1.5-inch position.

Figure 4-2

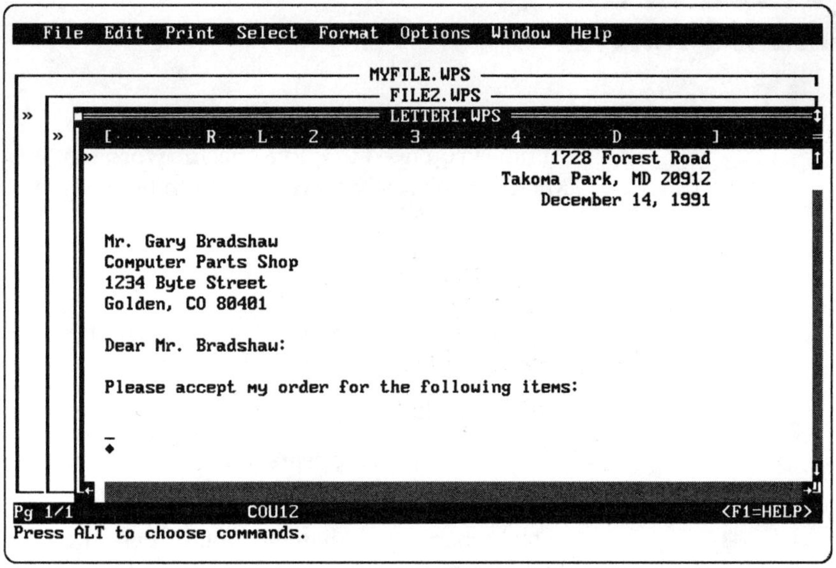

13. Press [Tab].

    The cursor jumps to the 5-inch position.

14. Type **$737.50.**

    The entry is made with the decimal point at the 5-inch position.

15. Press [Enter].

PRACTICE TIME

1. Type in the next two items.
2. Insert a blank line after the third item.
3. Set a left tab at the 3.5-inch position.
4. Enter the rest of the letter. (Closing appears at the 3.5-inch position.)

My check for $807.20 is enclosed.
Yours very truly,

<your name>
Enclosure

5. Perform the spelling check.
6. Save the letter again with the same filename.

FINDING TEXT

At times you need to find a specific word that is somewhere in the document. Microsoft Works has a command to help you do that.

1. Switch to MYFILE.
2. Position the cursor at the beginning of the file.

Pretend this is a long document and you need to find the word "cuneiform" because you have additional information you want to insert.

3. Select the Search... command from the Select menu.

   A dialog box appears as shown in Figure 4-3.

Works is asking you what text you want to find. It will find all occurrences of text (characters), disregarding upper- or lowercase. The text may even be embedded in another word. That is, if you want to search for "and," Works will find "hand," "band," or any other word that has the word "and" embedded in it. If you want Works to ignore such occurrences, you select the option Match Whole Word. If you want Works to pay attention to upper- and lowercase occurrence of the text, you select the second option, Match upper/lower case.

Figure 4-3

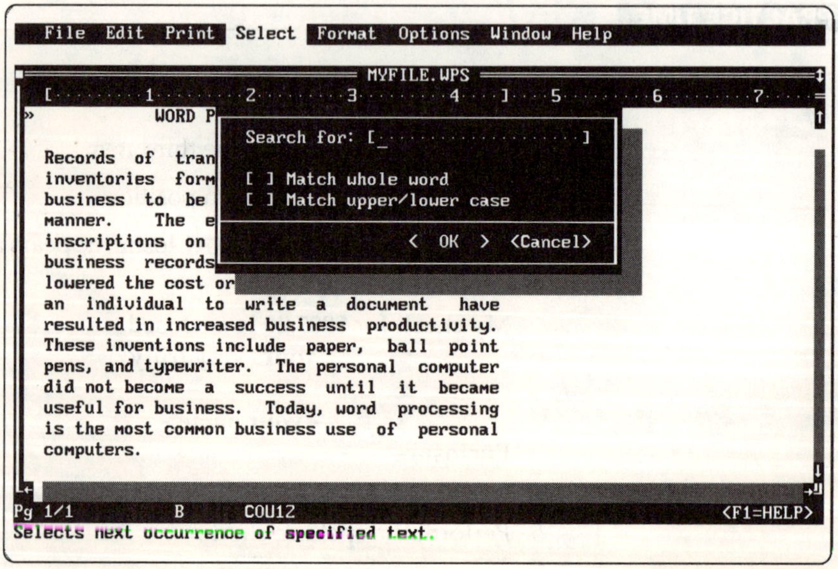

1. Type **cuneiform.**
2. Select the <OK> button.

   The word "cuneiform" is highlighted.

If you want to find the next occurrence of the same text, select the Search option from the Select menu and select <OK> again. The previous search criterion, cuneiform, is the default value. When there are no more occurrences in the text, you will get a dialog box informing you of this.

PRACTICE TIME

Find all occurrences of the word "productivity" in MYFILE.

*NOTE: When you choose Find from the Search menu, the word "cuneiform" will still appear as the search text. Therefore, type **productivity** and be sure the previous entry is erased.*

REPLACING WORDS

When editing a document, sometimes you want to find a particular word that needs to be replaced. For example, you might write a rather lengthy report on a client, only to find out that there has been a change in the client's company name. Rather than searching through the entire document visually, looking for the occurrence of the company name and replacing the name, you can use Works to find and replace it for you.

PRACTICE TIME

1. In this practice exercise you are going to create a new word processing document.
2. Enter the following text:

November 30, 1991

Mr. Smith
Personnel Office
Republic Engineering
3570 Fruitland Avenue
Maywood, OR 97119

Dear Mr. Smith:

I am applying for the draftsperson position advertised by Republic Engineering. My resume is enclosed. As you will notice, my background is very solid, just what Republic Engineering needs.

Another thing you will notice, Mr. Smith, is the loyalty I extend toward my employer. I have twice been selected as employee of the month. Republic Engineering is surely interested in such quality.

I look forward to hearing from you concerning an interview date and time. In the meanwhile, could you provide me with some information concerning the medical and retirement benefits available to Republic Engineering employees? Thank you.

Sincerely,

Michael Gregory

Encl.

3. Perform a spelling check; then save the letter as the file LETTER2.

You just found out that Mr. Smith is no longer with Republic Engineering. The letter has to be sent to Ms. Matthews.

1. Position the cursor at the beginning of the document.
2. Choose the Replace... command from the Select menu.

   The Replace dialog box is similar to the Search dialog box.
3. Type **Mr. Smith** and press [Tab].
4. Type **Ms. Matthews** and press [Tab].
5. Select the option to Match whole word.

If you were to select the Replace option, the first occurrence of "Mr. Smith" would be replaced by "Ms. Matthews." If you were to select Replace All, all occurrences of "Mr. Smith" would be replaced by "Ms. Matthews."

6. Select the Replace All option.

   A dialog box indicates that three occurrences have been replaced.

7. Select <OK>.

PRACTICE TIME

1. Replace all occurrences of Republic Engineering with Conway Architects.
2. Save the letter as LETTER3.
3. Close the file LETTER3.

PAGE BREAKS

When you have a multipage document, Works shows you where the printer will advance to a new page. These breaks are known as **soft page breaks** and are shown as a row of dots on the screen. As you look over the document, you may find that a soft page break occurs at an inappropriate place. For example, you do not want a page break to occur after printing just one line of a paragraph or in the middle of a table. In such a case, you need to enter a page break, known as a **hard page break,** manually. A hard page break is inserted by first positioning the insertion bar where you want the page break to occur and then choosing Insert Page Break from the Print menu.

1. Make MYFILE the active file.
2. Position the cursor on the blank line between two paragraphs.
3. Select the Insert Page Break command from the Print menu.

   The dotted line indicates a manual page break, as shown in Figure 4-4.

4. Print MYFILE.

   The document is printed on two pages.

Figure 4-4

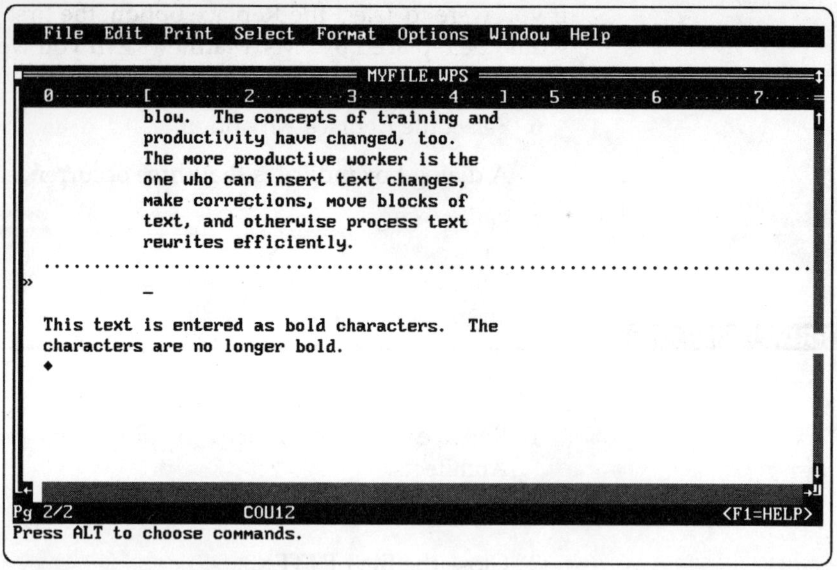

PRINTING PAGE NUMBERS

Works does not print page numbers by default. You may want the page number to appear at the top right of the page. You use the Headers & Footers... command from the Print menu to enter the appropriate commands in the Header and Footer boxes. The &P command tells Works to print the page number, and &R aligns following text at the right margin. You will enter the Header instruction &R&P.

NOTE: The on-screen help contains other options and examples. You can experiment on your own.

1. Select the Headers & Footers... command from the Print menu.
2. Type **&R&P** in the Header box.
3. Select the <OK> button.
4. Print the file again.

   The page numbers are printed in the upper right.

QUITTING THE SESSION

This is the end of this lesson. To quit properly, follow the instructions given in Lesson One. Save the changes to your files.

■ SUMMARY OF COMMANDS

Topic or Feature	*Command or Reference*	*Menu*	*Page*
Copying text	Copy	Edit	37
Moving text	Move	Edit	37
Entering text right justified	Right	Format	39
Setting left, right, center, or decimal tab stops	Tabs... Set alignment after selecting position	Format	40
Finding text	Search...	Select	42
Replacing text	Replace...	Select	43
Inserting a page break	Insert Page Break	Print	45
Printing page numbers	Headers & Footers... Enter &P command in header or footer box	Print	46

■ SELF-TEST

1. To copy text from one document to another, you first ___________ the text to be copied, then you select the ___________ command from the ___________ menu, and finally you position the cursor and press Enter.
2. To enter text right justified, you use the ___________ command from the ___________ menu.
3. You can set the following types of tab alignments: ___________, ___________, ___________, and ___________.
4. To locate a word or words in a document, you use the ___________ command from the ___________ menu.
5. To prevent locating words like "together" when searching for "get," you select the option ____________________.
6. To insert a page break in the text, you select the___________command from the ________________ menu.

LESSON FIVE

Spreadsheet: Creating a Simple Spreadsheet

OBJECTIVES

In this lesson you will learn how to:

- Understand spreadsheet terminology.
- Create a spreadsheet file.
- Select cells.
- Enter data into a spreadsheet file.
- Differentiate between text and number entries.
- Enter simple formulas.
- Save a file on a disk.
- Print a spreadsheet.

STARTING OFF

First, start up your computer and enter the Works program. Follow the instructions given in Lesson One. Insert your data disk into a disk drive.

STARTING A SPREADSHEET FILE

To create a spreadsheet file, do the following:

1. Select the Create New File... command from the File menu.
2. Select the <New Spreadsheet> option in the dialog box.

   An empty spreadsheet screen, as shown in Figure 5-1, is displayed.

At the top of the screen is the menu bar. On the top line of the work area, the default file name, SHEET1.WKS, appears. When you save the spreadsheet, you will give it a more descriptive name.

Figure 5-1

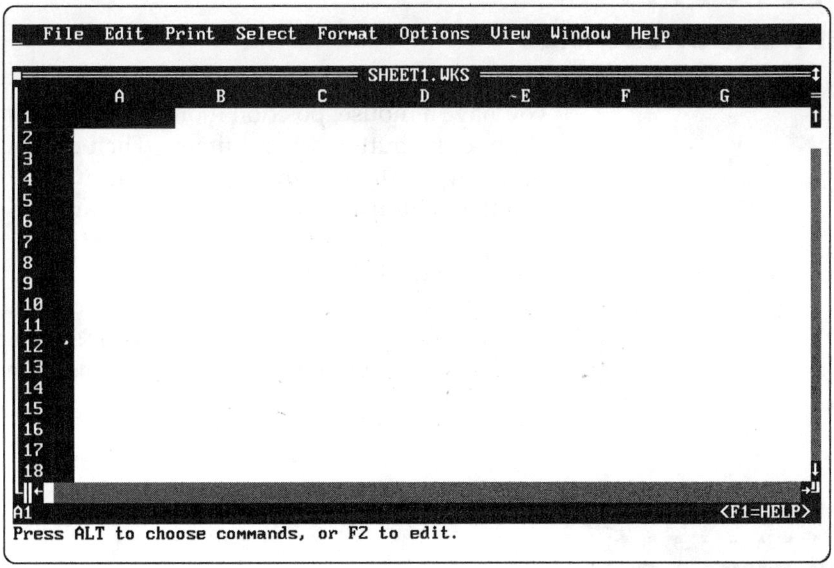

The work area is divided into rows and columns. Rows are numbered (for example, 1, 2, 3, and so on), and columns are lettered (for example, A, B, C, and so on). Each intersection of a column and a row (A1, B3, C17) is referred to as a **cell.**

ACTIVE CELL

Before you can enter data in a cell, the cell must be selected. The selected cell, which is highlighted, is referred to as the **active cell**. At the left edge of the status bar is the reference to the active cell, which is initially A1. The line below the menu bar is called the **formula bar** and displays the entries in the active cell.

There are several ways to move the highlight. You can use the arrow keys to move the highlight one row or column at a time, or you can use the mouse to point to a different cell and then press the left mouse button to select that cell.

PRACTICE TIME

Select various cells to make them active. Then select cell A1.

SPREADSHEET SIZE

If you have a mouse, position it on the down arrow on the vertical scroll bar and press the button several times. Then do the same several times on the right arrow of the horizontal scroll bar. If you do not have a mouse, hold down the right-arrow key until it repeats awhile; then hold down the down-arrow key similarly. Notice that the column and row headings change. The spreadsheet doesn't contain just 8 columns and up to 18 rows. There are 256 columns labeled A, B, C ... X, Y, Z, AA, AB, AC ... IV. Also, there are 4,096 rows. Because of the space limitation your screen imposes, however, you can see only a few rows and columns at any one time.

NOTE: The number of columns displayed depends on the column width.

FINDING A CELL

Suppose you want to select a particular cell to make it active, and also suppose this cell is not currently displayed on the screen. Rather than scrolling through the screen to locate it, you can use the Find Cell command.

1. Select the Go To... command from the Select menu.

   A dialog box is displayed, as shown in Figure 5-2.

Figure 5-2

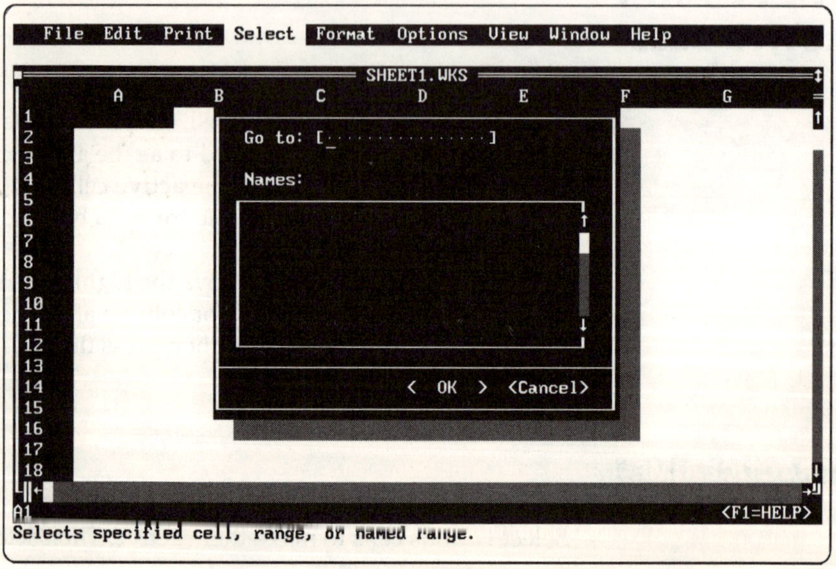

You want to select a particular cell.

2. Enter the cell coordinate you want to make active, say **H21**, in the Go To box.
3. Select the <OK> box.

   The cell H21 appears on the screen and has been made active.

PRACTICE TIME

1. Make cell C75 active.
2. Make cell F23 active.
3. When you are satisfied that you can make any cell active, select cell A1 again.

ENTERING DATA

The entry you make at a cell is text, a number, or a formula. A **text** entry is a combination of character(s) or word(s), and is not used in calculations. An example of text entry is a heading, known as a **label,** that is needed so that you can later identify what other entries on the same row or column stand for. **Number** entries are values that can be used for calculations. Text entries are displayed left justified and numbers are displayed right justified in the cell. **Formula** entries, discussed a little later, are entries that, when evaluated, yield numbers which are displayed in their cells.

Text and numbers are known as **constant values**. To enter a constant value, you select a cell and type the entry. Works determines whether an entry is text or a number on the basis of the first character you enter.

- If the first character is a letter (A to Z), Works assumes that you are entering a text.
- If the first character is a digit (0 to 9), a decimal point, a plus (+) or minus (–) sign, or another special character (special characters are not discussed here), the program assumes that you are typing in a number.

NOTE: If you want to begin a text entry with a number, type a quotation mark (") first and then enter the text. The quotation mark is a signal to Works that you're typing a text entry. The character appears in the entry bar but not in the cell.

Uppercase Characters

To make an uppercase character in your text entry, hold Shift down while you press the character, just as you would do on a typewriter. If you want to type the entire entry in uppercase letters, press Caps Lock once. To type lowercase letters again, simply press Caps Lock again. When entering shifted nonalphabetic characters, you need to hold Shift down even if Caps Lock is active.

As you type the entry, it appears on the formula bar. If you notice an error, you can press Backspace to back up and make corrections. When you finish typing the entry, you should visually verify the entry as displayed on the formula bar before completing the entry. Methods of completing the entry are discussed later in this lesson.

PREPARING THE SPREADSHEET

You will learn the various features of the Works spreadsheet through an example. You will help Susan, who has started a new business and wants to keep track of her income and expenses using a spreadsheet. She wants to find out what her profit is each day.

You will start by setting up the spreadsheet for just the first day. In the next two lessons, you will add more entries and expand and modify the spreadsheet.

ENTERING TEXT

First, you will label the rows. That is, you will enter texts that explain what data are entered in the rows. You will use the labels "Income" for income, "Expense" for expenses, and "Profit" for profit. If the label you are entering is too long to fit in one cell, Microsoft Works automatically runs the label and displays each section in blank adjacent cells.

Completing an Entry

An entry into a cell is completed by any of the following procedures:

- Pressing Enter or an arrow key.
- Pressing Tab, Home, End, Pg Up, or Pg Dn.
- Moving the cursor using the mouse.

Correcting Errors

We all make mistakes. If you notice an error after completing an entry, you can do one of the following procedures to correct it:

- Reenter the information by selecting the cell containing the error and then entering the correct data.
- If you made an entry in a wrong cell, erase the entry by using the Clear command. That is, select the cell to be erased, and then choose Clear from the Edit menu.

1. Select cell A1.
2. Type the word **Income** (do not press Enter).

   What you type appears on the formula bar and in the active cell, as shown in Figure 5-3.

Figure 5-3

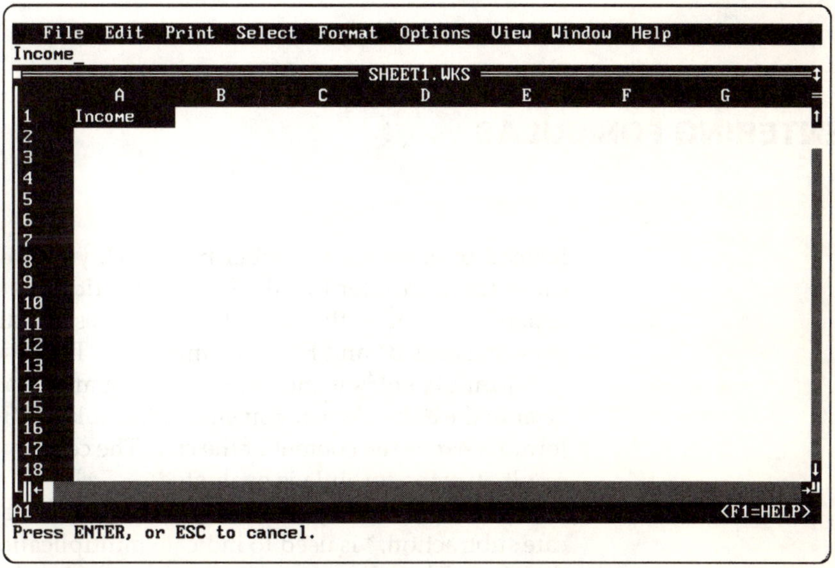

3. Press Enter to complete the entry.
4. Select cell A2, type the label **Expense,** and press Enter.

PRACTICE TIME

1. Enter the label **Profit** at cell A3.
2. Select cell B1.

ENTERING NUMBERS

Susan earns $600 the first day, and she spends $400 in advertising expenses. Enter these values in the spreadsheet.

1. With cell B1 selected, enter the value **600**.

   The number 600 appears right justified in cell B1.

2. Select cell B2.

PRACTICE TIME

Enter the value **400** in cell B2.

ENTERING FORMULAS

Instead of entering a number in cell B3, you will enter a formula that will cause the computer to calculate the Profit. The formula is "income minus expense." That is, the formula determines the difference between numbers stored in cells B1 and B2, or B1 minus B2. The result is displayed in cell B3.

A formula entry is indicated by using an equals sign (=) as the first character in the entry. When you enter a formula, the formula itself appears in the formula bar as the content of the cell. The cell, however, displays the numeric result after the formula is evaluated.

In a formula, the operator + is used to indicate addition, – is used to indicate subtraction, * is used to indicate multiplication, and / is used to indicate division. These operators are evaluated from left to right. As in ordinary mathematics, multiplication and division take precedence over addition and subtraction unless the latter operations are enclosed in parentheses. For example, =6 + 4/2 results in 8, whereas = (6 + 4)/2 yields 5.

Returning to helping Susan start her business, the formula for Profit is =B1–B2.

1. Select cell B3, type **=B1–B2,** and then press Enter.

   The formula bar shows the content as =B1–B2.

   Cell B3 shows the number 200, which is the result of evaluating the expression (600–400).

2. In cell B2, enter any number other than 400—for instance, 250.

Did you notice what happened to the number at B3? If you missed it, enter another number at cell B2.

The number in B3 changes.

The computer saves the formula for the value displayed at B3. This cell always displays the result of the expression =B1–B2. Thus, the computer recalculates B3 every time you change the values in B1 or B2.

Are you beginning to see the power of a spreadsheet?

As you entered this formula, you may have had to check for the coordinates of cells displaying the values for Income and Expenses. Had this been a large spreadsheet, you might have had trouble determining which cell contains which value. If the cells you wanted had scrolled off the screen, you would have had to scroll to find them. After finding them, you would have had to note their positions, select the cell in which you wanted to enter the formula, and then type the formula. The spreadsheet program can make this process a little easier.

1. Erase the entry at cell B3 by selecting cell B3 and then selecting Clear from the Edit menu.

   Cell B3 clears.

Now, to enter the formula.

2. Press the = key (do not press [Enter]).

   = appears on the formula bar and in cell B3.

3. Select cell B1, where value for income appears, by using the arrow keys or the mouse.

   The formula bar and cell B3 now read =B1.

4. Press [-].

   The formula bar and cell B3 read =B1–.

Now, enter the second part of the formula by selecting the cell that contains the value for expense.

5. Select cell B2, where the value for the Expense appears.

   The formula bar and cell B3 now read =B1–B2.

6. Press [Enter] to complete the entry.

You can see that pointing to (selecting) cells has the same effect as typing those cell coordinates directly from the keyboard.

7. Enter the value **400** at B2.

PRACTICE TIME

1. Susan decides that 25 percent of her profit should go toward purchasing new equipment. Enter the label **Equipment** in cell A4. In cell B4, enter a formula for evaluating the amount to be spent on equipment. The formula is 0.25 of the value in cell B3, or =.25*B3.
2. Susan wants to know her net profit after purchasing equipment. In row 5 enter the label **-Net-** and the formula used to calculate it. The formula for Net is Profit minus Equipment, or =B3–B4. Your screen should look like Figure 5-4.

Figure 5-4

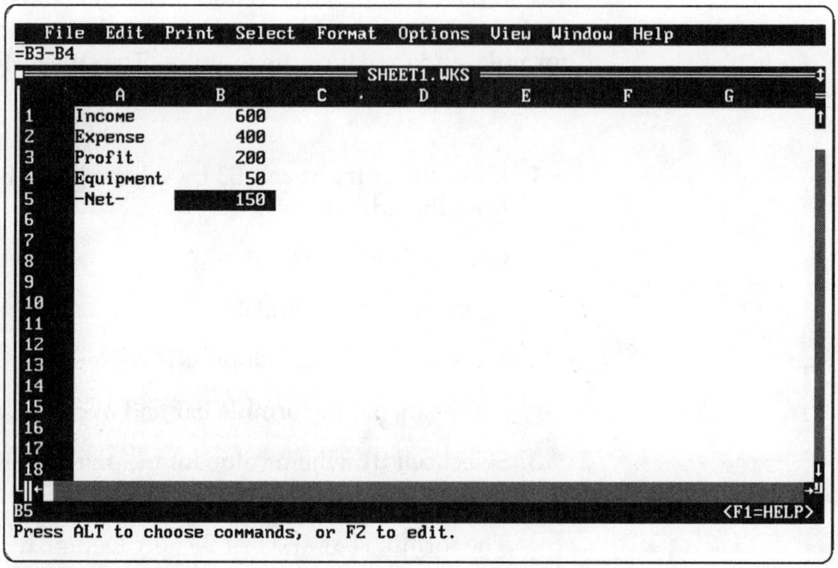

SAVING YOUR WORK

The spreadsheet you see is stored in the main memory of the computer. When you turn the computer off, all the information will be gone. Usually, you develop a spreadsheet in one or more sessions and then use it again in subsequent sessions. Thus, it is important to save the spreadsheet by some convenient means. You will save the spreadsheet as a file named MONEY.

1. Select the Save As... command from the File menu.

   A dialog box appears, with the original name, SHEET1.WKS, selected.

2. Select the drive containing your data disk in the Directories box and then select the <OK> button.

3. Enter **MONEY** in the filename box and then select the <OK> button.

   Works saves the spreadsheet as a new file on the disk and changes the name on the status line.

   You return to the spreadsheet.

PRINTING THE SPREADSHEET

Now, print the spreadsheet using the Print command.

1. Make sure that the printer is turned on and is ready for use.

2. Select the Print... command from the Print menu.

   A dialog box is displayed as shown in Figure 5-5.

Figure 5-5

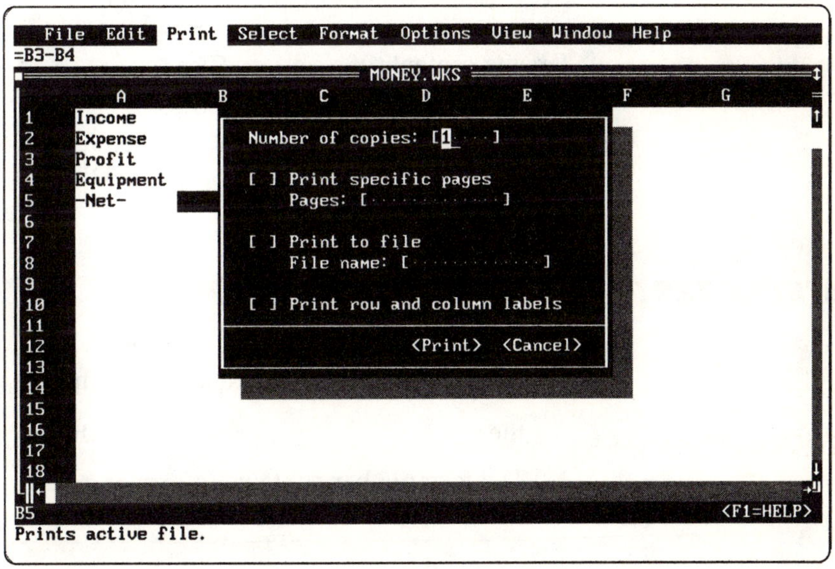

NOTE: If the dialog box on your screen does not have the same options as shown in Figure 5-5, set the options so that they are the same.

3. Select the PRINT command.

   Your spreadsheet is printed.

NOTE: If you want to cancel printing, press Esc.

If your printout looks good, you are done with this lesson. If it doesn't, go back and fix your spreadsheet. After you make corrections, save your work using the Save command and print it again.

QUITTING THE SESSION

This is the end of this lesson. To quit properly, follow the instructions given in Lesson One.

SUMMARY OF COMMANDS

Topic or Feature	*Command or Reference*	*Menu*	*Page*
Moving cell highlight	Arrow keys, mouse, scroll bars		49
Erasing contents of a cell	Clear	Edit	55
Finding a cell	Go To...	Select	50
Saving a file	Save, Save As...	File	56
Printing a spreadsheet	Print...	Print	57

SELF-TEST

1. To select a particular cell without scrolling through the spreadsheet, use the ______________ command from the ______________ menu option.
2. The formula bar contains information on ______________________________.
3. To complete an entry for a cell, you can either ______________ or ______________.
4. An entry is text if it begins with a letter or ______________.

5. An entry is a formula if it begins with ______________________.

6. To enter text that begins with a number, ______________________.

7. To move the highlight (change the selected cell) without using a menu option, you can either use arrow keys or ______________________.

8. In a formula, addition is represented by _____; subtraction, by _____; multiplication, by _____; and division, by _____.

9. To erase an entry, you select the cell and then select the ______________ command from the ______________ menu.

10. To print a spreadsheet, you select the ______________ command from the ______________ menu.

LESSON SIX

Spreadsheet: Expanding and Formatting the Simple Spreadsheet

OBJECTIVES

In this lesson you will learn how to:

- Retrieve a spreadsheet file from a disk.
- Insert a row.
- Specify a range.
- Change the display format of a text entry.
- Change column width.
- Use a function.
- Right-justify a text entry.
- Save a file using a different filename.

STARTING OFF

Start your computer and enter the Works program so that the initial screen is displayed. Insert your data disk from Lesson Five into a disk drive.

First you will retrieve the spreadsheet from what you created in the last lesson.

1. Select the Open Existing File... command from the File menu.
2. In the Directories box, select the drive containing your data disk and press Enter.
3. In the Files box, select MONEY.WKS displayed under Spreadsheet files.

   The spreadsheet from Lesson Five is displayed on the screen, as shown in Figure 6-1.

Figure 6-1

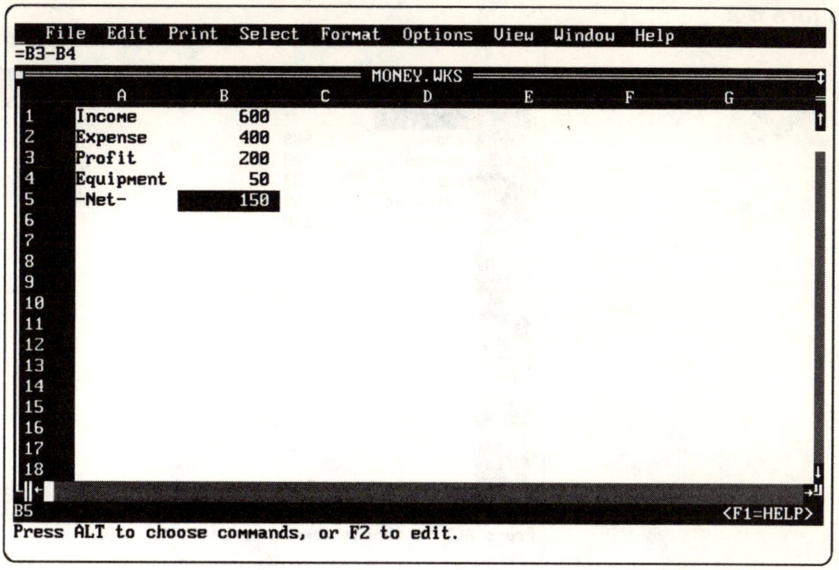

INSERT COMMAND

Right now, your spreadsheet shows values for Income, Expense, Profit, Equipment, and Net for 1 day. You will now extend these entries to show 10 days of business activity. You will enter the figures for the second day in column C, for the third day in column D, and so on. To identify the values easily, you will enter headings for these columns.

The column headings should go on row 1. Do you see a problem? Row 1 already has some entries. You could erase the whole spreadsheet and start over again, putting income in row 2, expense in row 3, profit in row 4, and so on. However, there is an easier way. You can insert a row at row 1.

1. Select row 1 by positioning the mouse and pressing the left button or by using the arrow keys.
2. Select the Insert Row/Column command from the Edit menu.

   A dialog box appears.
3. Select Row and then select the <OK> button.

   All the information on the spreadsheet moves down one row, and row 1 is now blank, as shown in Figure 6-2.

Let's proceed with labeling the columns.

Figure 6-2

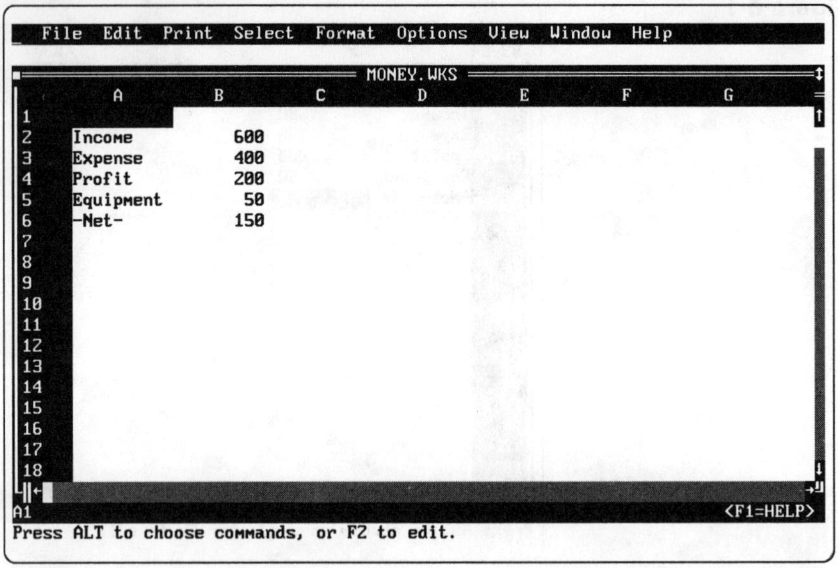

4. Select cell A1 and enter the label **Day.**

5. Select cell B1 and enter **1.**

Now, you need to enter 2 at C1, 3 at D1, ..., 10 at K1. To do so, select cell C1 and enter 2, select cell D1 and enter 3, and so on. But try a different way. Each entry is 1 greater than the previous one. The entry in C1 is the entry in B1 plus 1; the entry in D1 is the entry in C1 plus 1; and so on. So, you can enter the formula =B1+1 at C1, =C1+1 at D1, and so on.

6. Select cell C1 and enter **=B1+1.**

   The number 2 is displayed at C1.

Think for a moment. You will have to enter the formula =C1+1 at cell D1, =D1+1 at cell E1, and so on up to J1+1 at K1. It is tedious to enter nearly the same formula over and over. In this case, you need to do this only nine times. But what if you were setting up the spreadsheet for a month or a year?

FILL RIGHT COMMAND

There is an easier way to complete the spreadsheet. Use the Fill Right command from the Edit menu. You can use this command to make copies of formulas, texts, numbers, and blank entries across a row.

1. Select cells C1 through K1 by holding down the mouse button or holding down [Shift] while you move the arrow keys to select the cells.
2. Select Fill Right from the Edit menu.

   Numbers appear in columns D through K, as shown in Figure 6-3.

Figure 6-3

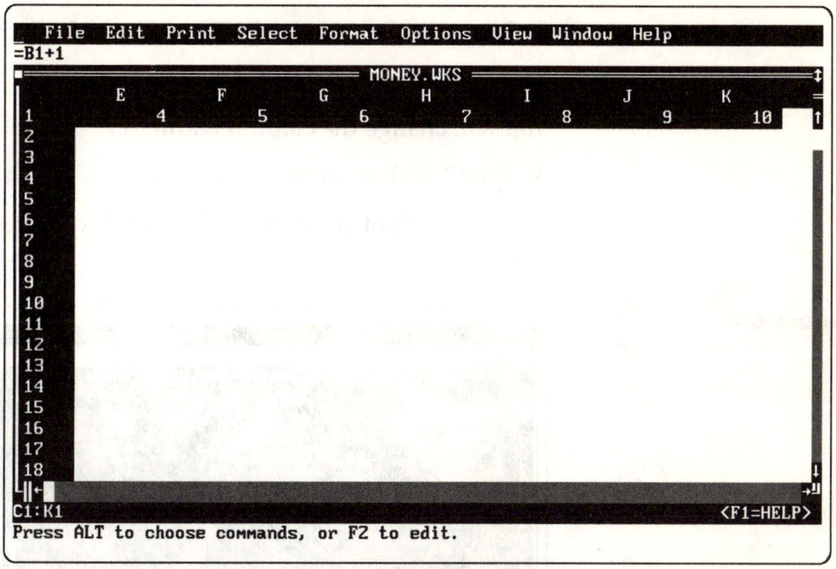

3. Move the highlight along row 1. Notice the contents of each cell as displayed on the formula bar.

As the formula =B1+1 was copied to cells D1 through K1, the cell coordinate changed for each cell. That is, the formula is =B1+1 in cell C1, =C1+1 in cell D1, and so on, just as you wanted. The formula =B1+1 gave a **relative reference** for a cell address rather than an **absolute reference.** A relative reference gives general directions to Works. In this case, the formula simply said add 1 to the contents of the cell to the left and display the result. That was the formula that was copied all the way across. An absolute reference would have given the specific cell coordinate. To give an absolute reference, you enter the formula with $ (dollar sign) preceding the cell's column label and row number. For example, if you want the formula =B1+1 to appear in all the cells, you enter =B1+1.

CHANGING COLUMN WIDTH

Initially, every column in the spreadsheet is 10 characters wide; that is, 10 characters are displayed at each coordinate. You can make the column up to 79 characters wide.

You change the width of a column by choosing Column Width... from the Format menu. You can also change the width of several consecutive columns or the entire spreadsheet with one command. You will now change the width of columns A through K.

1. Select cells A1 through K1.
2. Select the Column Width... command from the Format menu.

   A dialog box appears.

You will change the column width to 7.

3. Type **7** and select the <OK> button.

   The width of columns A through K changes to 7, as shown in Figure 6-4.

Figure 6-4

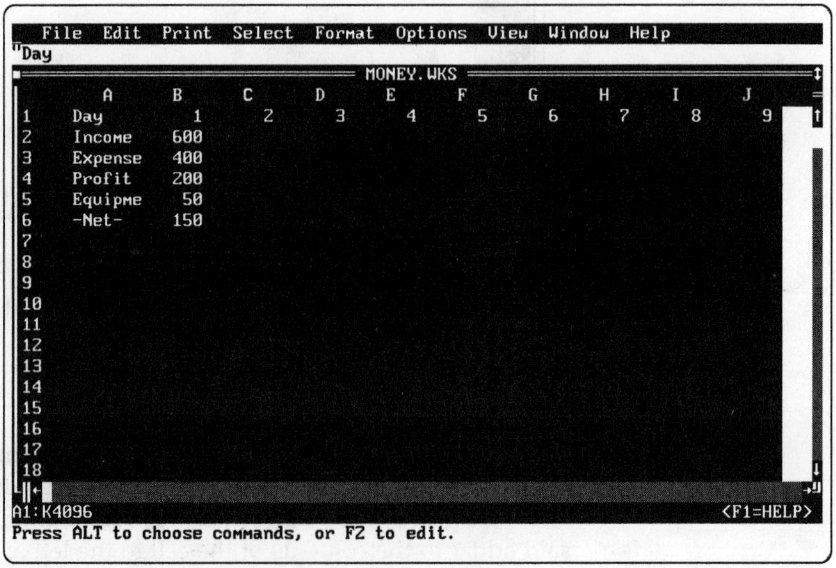

You can change the width of one column, column A, by selecting any cell in column A and following the steps just described.

1. Select a cell in column A.
2. Select the Column Width command in the Format menu.
3. Set the width to 11.

   The width of column A is set to 11.

NOTE: When you change the width of a column, the values or the text stored are not affected. The change affects only the number of characters displayed on the spread sheet. If a value is too large to be displayed within the specified column width, the cell displays #s. If text is too long to be displayed within the specified column width, Works automatically runs the label and displays each section in blank adjacent cells.

PRACTICE TIME

1. Decrease the width of column B to 2. Notice that cells B2, B3, B4, B5, and B6 fill with #s.
2. Change the width of column B to 7.
3. Enter the following values for days 2 through 5.

Day	2	3	4	5
Income	300	950	1000	692.50
Expense	275	500	500	600.34

4. Use the Fill Right command to copy the formulas for Profit, Equipment, and Net, as entered in cells B4, B5, and B6, into the ranges C4 through K4, C5 through K5, and C6 through K6, respectively, as shown in Figure 6-5.

Figure 6-5

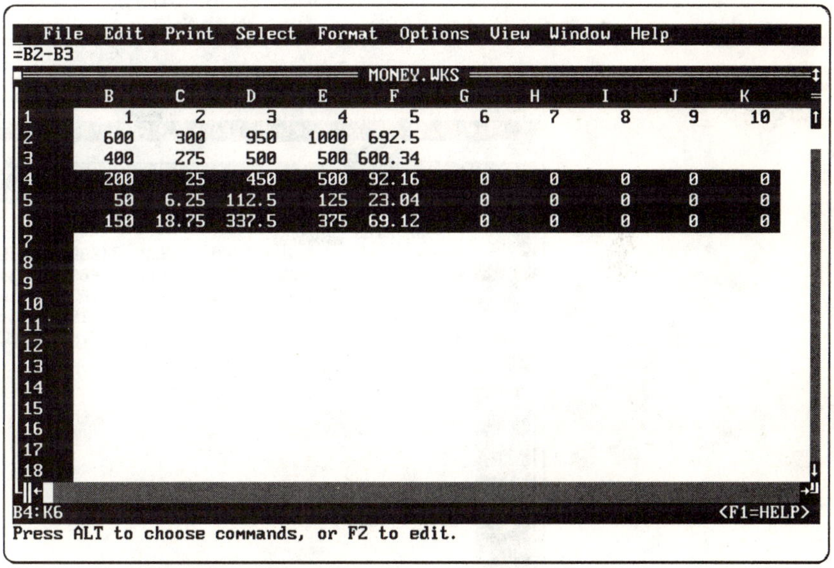

Now, Susan can see the profitability of the business at a glance. Columns G through K are blank for "income" and "expense" rows and show 0 (zero) for the rest. These columns are already set up, so that as Susan enters values for income and expense on days 6 through 10, profit, equipment, and net will be calculated and displayed automatically.

NOTE: It is possible to set up an entire spreadsheet without data. It can contain all the headings and formulas needed, have all columns set to proper width, and have the display format specified. Such a spreadsheet is called a ***template****. A template is a prewritten spreadsheet that is ready to accept data. All one has to do to use a template is to retrieve it and enter data into the proper cells.*

It occurs to Susan at this point that she started her business with a certain amount of cash—call it Cash-on-Hand. She would like to see the change in that value from day to day. She decides that she would like to see this figure in row 2.

PRACTICE TIME

1. Insert a blank row at row 2.
2. Enter the row heading **Cash-on-Hand** in cell A2.
3. If needed, adjust the width of column A so that the heading fits.
4. Enter the value **750** in cell B2 as the starting value.

Your screen should look similar to Figure 6-6.

Figure 6-6

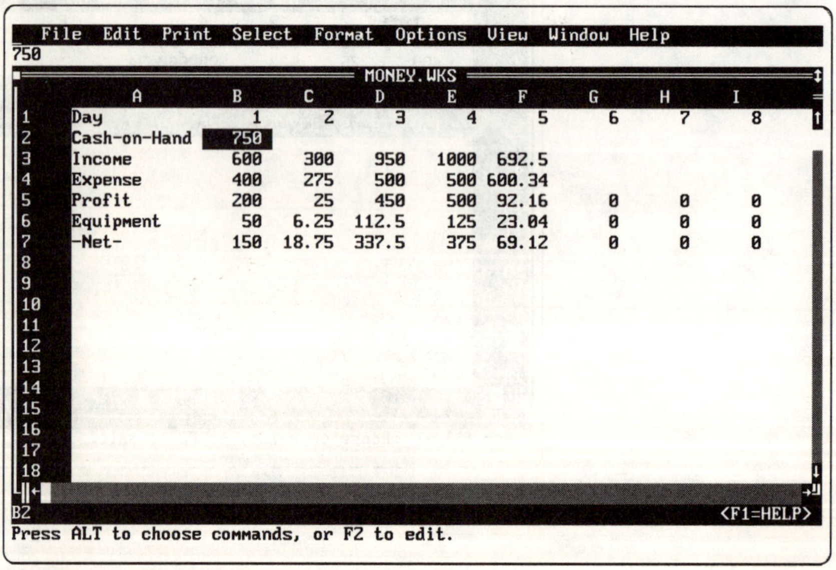

Think about this for a minute. The value for Cash-on-Hand changes daily depending on the net profit. On the second day the Cash-on-Hand is the sum of the Cash-on-Hand for the first day plus the net profit for the first day. So, the formula used for Cash-on-Hand for the second day is the value at cell B2 plus the value at cell B7.

PRACTICE TIME

1. Enter the formula for Cash-on-Hand for the second day.
2. Use the Fill Right command to copy this formula to the range D2 through K2, as shown in Figure 6-7.

Cash-on-Hand values for days 6 through 10 remain constant since net values are zero for those days.

Figure 6-7

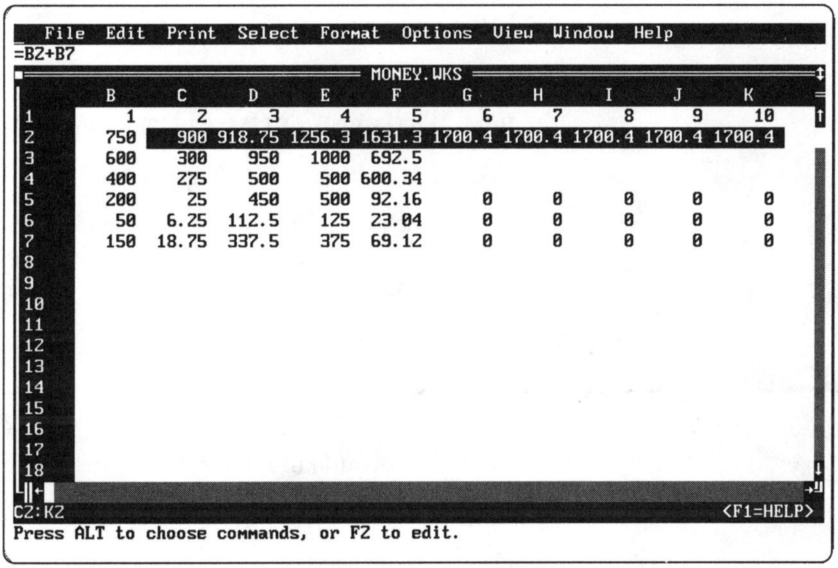

SUM FUNCTION

For column L, Susan decides that she would like to see totals for income, expense, profit, equipment, and net for the 10-day period. To enter the total income at L3, for instance, you could enter the formula =B3+C3+D3+E3+F3+G3+H3+I3+J3+K3. That's a long formula. Suppose you had to find the total income for 60 days? As you might have guessed, there is an easier way to total numbers. You can use the SUM function.

A function is a built-in calculation. A SUM function will give you the sum of things you specify, called **arguments.** The arguments can be any of the following:

- A number—a specific value, such as 5 or 246.

- A formula—an expression that, when evaluated, gives a number, such as 8/3.
- A cell reference—the coordinate of a cell whose content you want added, such as A17 or G92.
- A range reference—coordinates of a range of cells whose contents you want added. A range is a rectangular section of a spreadsheet. You reference a range by specifying the coordinates of top left and bottom right corner cells of the range, separated by a colon (:)—for example, A7:A15 or C1:E5.
- Another function.

To use the SUM function, perform the following steps.

1. Select cell L3.
2. Enter the formula **=SUM(B3:K3)** and press [Enter].

   In cell L3, the value 3542.5 appears.

You could have specified the range using the mouse or arrow keys. All you had to do was to enter **=SUM(**, then select cells B2 through K2, type **)**, and press [Enter].

PRACTICE TIME

1. Copy the formula in L3 to cells L4 through L7.

Hint: Select cells L3 through L7; then select the Fill Down from the Edit menu.

2. Enter the label **TOTAL** in cell L1, as shown in Figure 6-8.

JUSTIFYING TEXT ENTRY

Does anything about the label you just entered bother you? It doesn't line up above all the values for the total. Also, there is no space between it and the heading 10 in column K. The reason is that values are displayed right justified, whereas labels are displayed left justified in the spreadsheet. You can change the label format for this cell alone so that it is right justified.

1. Select cell L1.
2. Select the Style... command from the Format menu.

   A dialog box appears.

Figure 6-8

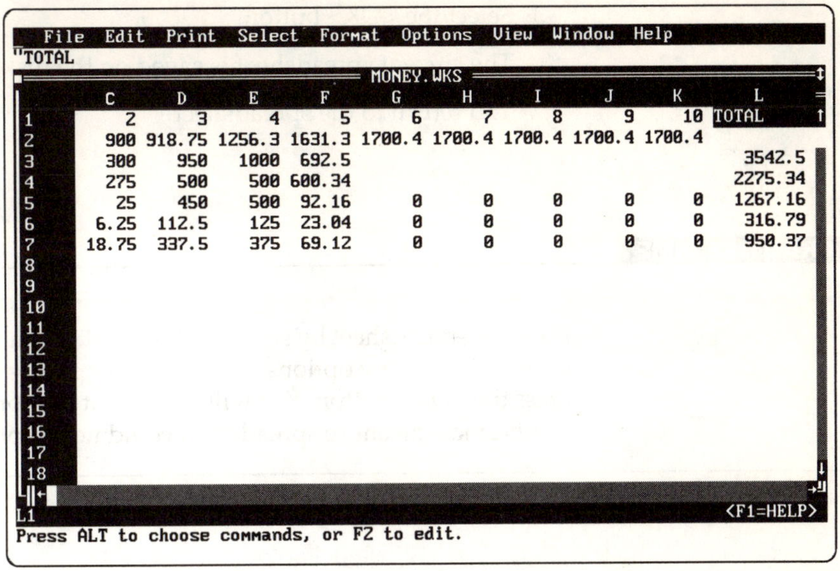

In the Alignment box, various options are displayed.

3. Select Right in the Alignment box; then select the <OK> button.

   The word "TOTAL" is displayed right justified at cell L1.

SAVING A FILE USING A DIFFERENT FILENAME

This is the end of another lesson. Save your spreadsheet for use during the next lesson. When you save the spreadsheet, however, be careful in choosing the filename.

If you use the same filename you did at the end of the last lesson, the current spreadsheet will replace the existing contents of the disk file. This may be acceptable in some situations. By using a different filename, however, both the old and new spreadsheets will be stored on the disk. As you learned in Lesson One, you use the Save As... command to save the spreadsheet with a different name.

You will save the spreadsheet using a different filename since the spreadsheets from this and the previous lesson will be used in the next lesson.

1. Select the Save As... command from the File menu.

   The Save As dialog box appears, with the original name MONEY displayed.

2. Type **MONEY2.**

3. Select the <OK> button.

   The current spreadsheet is saved on the disk.

   You return to the spreadsheet.

PRACTICE TIME

Print the spreadsheet by selecting the Print... command from the Print menu. Do not change any options. A dialog box appears indicating a printing error. Press the <OK> button. You will notice that the spreadsheet is printed on two sheets since the entire spreadsheet could not be printed on one sheet.

QUITTING THE SESSION

This is the end of this lesson. Quit the session as described in Lesson One.

SUMMARY OF COMMANDS

Topic or Feature	*Command or Reference*	*Menu*	*Page*
Inserting a row or column	Insert Row/Column	Edit	61
Copying a formula into cells to the right	Fill Right	Edit	63
Copying a formula into cells beneath	Fill Down	Edit	68
Changing column width	Select columns, then Column Width...	Format	64
Justifying text entries	Style... Select General, Left, Right, or Center	Format	68
Saving file to disk	Save, Save As...	File	69
Printing file	Print...	Print	70

■ SELF-TEST

1. What is the function that is equivalent to the formula =B1+C1+C2+C3?

   ____________________.

2. What is the difference between a relative reference and an absolute reference? ____.

3. When number signs (#) are displayed in a cell, this means that ________________________.

4. How do you go about changing the width of just one column? ________________________________.

5. How do you change the column width of several consecutive columns? ____.

6. What does Fill Right do? ________________________________.

7. What is an argument in a function? ____________________________.

8. To right-justify text in a cell, select that cell and then select the ______________ command from the ______________ menu.

9. What happens when you save a file the second time using the same filename? ____.

10. What happens when a spreadsheet is too wide to print on one page? ____.

LESSON SEVEN

Spreadsheet: Modifying the Display Format

OBJECTIVES

In this lesson you will learn how to:

- Change the display format for the entire spreadsheet or for selected cells.
- Move information within the spreadsheet.
- Delete columns.
- Display formulas that were entered in the spreadsheet.
- Move information from one spreadsheet to another.
- Switch from one file to another.

STARTING OFF

Start your computer and enter the Works program so that the Open dialog box is displayed. Insert the data disk from Lesson Six into a disk drive. Retrieve the spreadsheet file, MONEY2, which you saved at the end of the last lesson.

CHANGING THE DISPLAY FORMAT

You can improve the readability of the spreadsheet by changing the display format. You can change the format of the entire spreadsheet or of selected cells only by using the Format menu command.

Bold Characters

Headings on the spreadsheet can be made to stand out by displaying them in bold characters.

1. Select cells A1 through L1 by using the mouse or by pressing [Shift] while using the arrow keys.
2. Select the Style... command from the Format menu option.

   A dialog box appears, as shown in Figure 7-1.

Figure 7-1

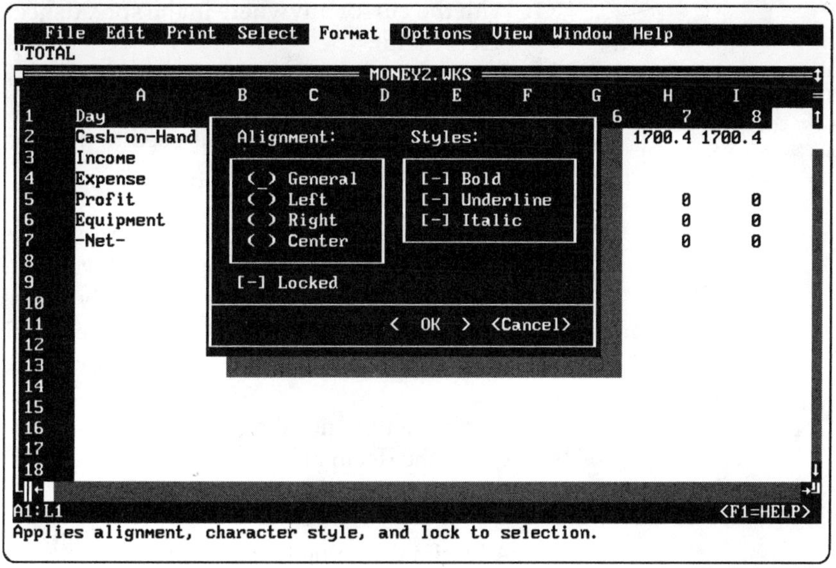

This dialog box displays several options. It lets you set the alignment of the selected cells, and it lets you select whether the cells are displayed in bold, underlined, or in italics.

3. Move the cursor to the Bold option in the Styles box.
4. Press [Spacebar].

   An X appears in the box.
5. Select the <OK> button.

   The column headings are displayed in bold characters.

To change the style back to normal, you go through the same procedure. This time, the X disappears from the box. The attributes—bold, underline, and italics—are **toggled,** or turned on and off by successive selections of those boxes.

PRACTICE TIME

Display the row headings in column A in bold.

Display Format of Numbers

You can make the entire spreadsheet display whole numbers (no numbers to the right of the decimal point). Note that some of the values in the spreadsheet have decimal values.

1. With the cursor anywhere in the spreadsheet, select the All option in the Select menu.

   The entire spreadsheet is highlighted.

You want to change the format used to display numbers.

2. Select the Format menu option.

The box beginning with the General format contains the display formats. Initially, the entire spreadsheet is displayed in the General format, which means a number is displayed as accurately as possible, given the cell width. For example, if you type 12345.6789, the display may show 12345.6789, 12345.7, 12346, 1E+4 (scientific), and so on, depending on the width of the cell.

To display whole numbers, you specify Fixed format with zero places to the right of the decimal.

1. Select the Fixed... option.

   A Decimals dialog box appears.

2. In the dialog box, enter **0** and select the <OK> button.

   The decimal portions of the numbers are dropped, as shown in Figure 7-2.

Figure 7-2

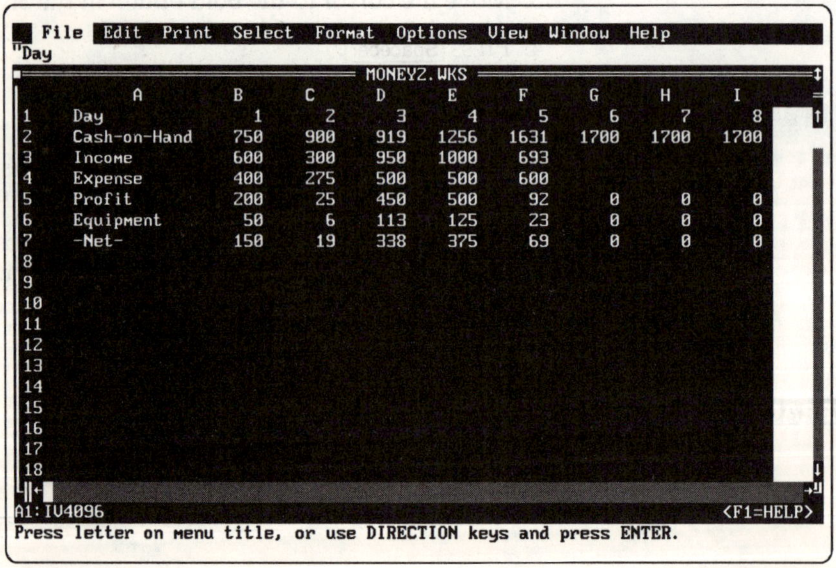

Since this spreadsheet shows dollar amounts, you probably want to change the format to show two places to the right of the decimal point. You could use the Dollar... format, but suppose that you don't want dollar signs. You can use the Fixed... format with two places to the right of the decimal.

PRACTICE TIME

Change the format for the entire spreadsheet so that amounts will be displayed with two places to the right of the decimal point. You will need to change the widths of columns E through L to 8. When done, your screen should look similar to Figure 7-3.

Figure 7-3

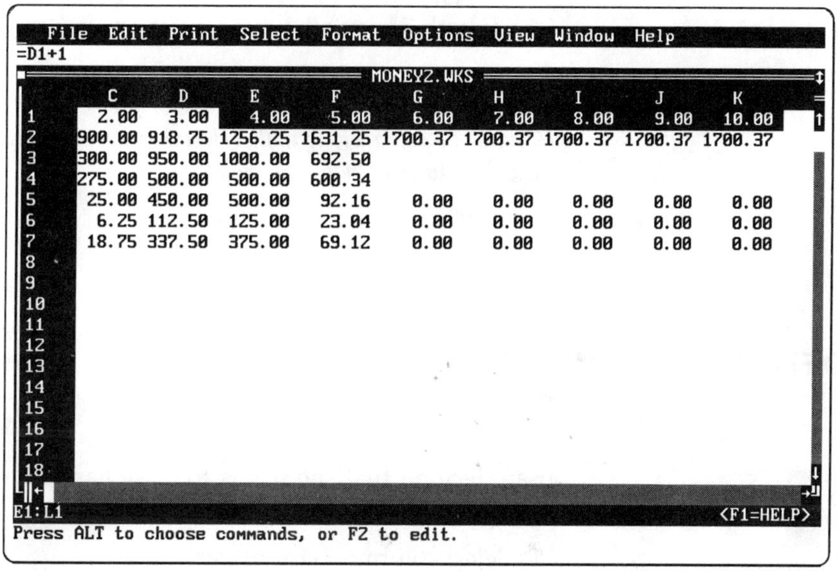

All values on the screen now have two places to the right of the decimal. Do you see a problem? Even the column headings have two decimal places. Since these headings signify day 1, day 2, and so on, they should be whole numbers.

PRACTICE TIME

Change the display format of B1 through K1 to Fixed with zero decimal places.

MOVING INFORMATION IN A SPREADSHEET

Susan just decided that she would like to see the values for Cash-on-Hand displayed as the last items on the spreadsheet, not the first. You can reenter the entries in rows 2 in row 8 and then remove row 2. However, it is easier to use the Move command.

1. Select row 2.
2. Select the Move command from the Edit menu.

   The message line instructs you to select the new location and press [Enter].
3. Select row 8.
4. Press [Enter].

   The entries in row 2 have moved to row 7 and the entries in rows 3 through 7 have all moved up one row.

NOTE: When you Copy entries, the original cells are left unchanged. The Move command, by contrast, actually relocates the values and adjusts any references in the spreadsheet to cells that were moved.

DELETING COLUMNS

Susan decided that she wants to close her spreadsheet now. She wants to delete columns for days 6 through 10.

1. Select columns G through K.
2. Select the Delete command from the Edit menu.

   The screen changes to Figure 7-4.
3. Select cell G2.

   The entry line shows the content as:

```
=SUM(ERR).
```

The formula had been =SUM(B2:K2), but when column K was deleted, the formula did not adjust.

Figure 7-4

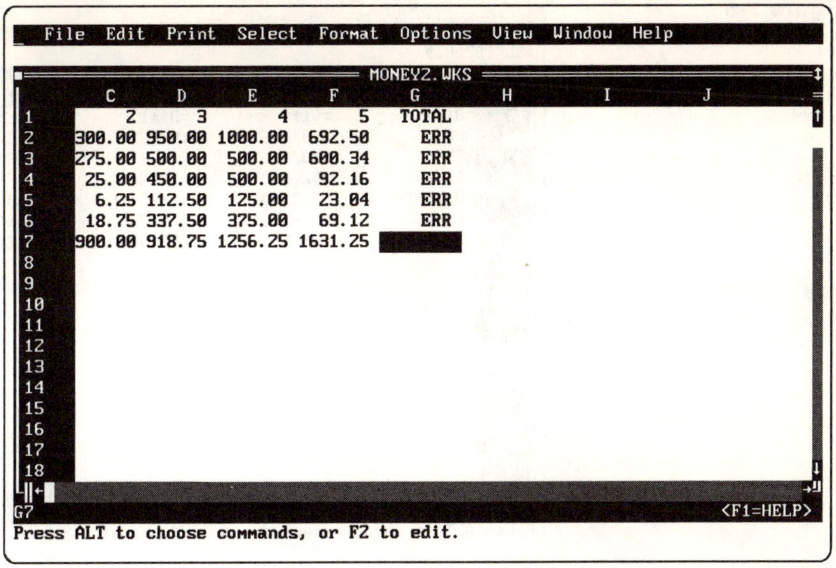

PRACTICE TIME

Use F2 to edit each entry, and correct the entries in column G. For example, at G2 the argument should be B2:F2. Change the width of column G to 9 so all the numbers are displayed.

FORMULA DISPLAY

When you choose the Print command from the Print menu, an image of what is displayed on the screen is printed on the paper. It is very difficult for someone else to tell by looking at the printout whether you entered a value or a formula to obtain the number displayed at a cell.

Even when you are looking at a spreadsheet on the screen, unless you select a particular cell (and look at the cell content), it is not possible to tell whether what is displayed is an actual value or result of a formula.

You can have Works display what was actually entered (whether it is a value or a formula) at each cell.

1. Select the Show Formulas command from the Options menu.

   A check mark appears in front of Show Formulas.

   The display changes and is similar to Figure 7-5.

NOTE: You may have to adjust the column width to accommodate formula display.

Figure 7-5

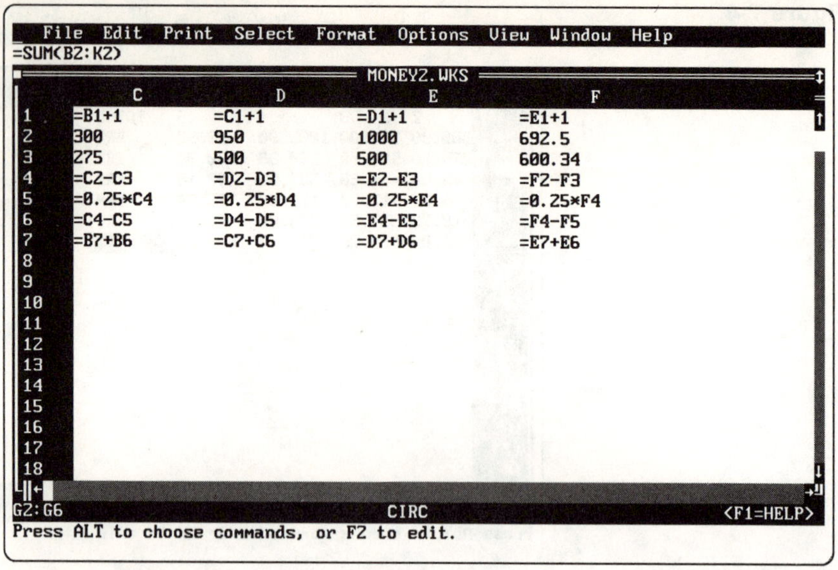

At all cells where values were entered, the entry that was typed (whether it is a number or a formula) is displayed. Look through the whole spreadsheet. You can see right away what was entered at each coordinate. You can get a printout of this formula display in the usual way.

You return to the initial display option by again choosing Show Formulas from the Options menu.

2. Select the Show Formulas command from the Options menu.

   The screen display returns to its initial display mode.

PRACTICE TIME

1. Change to Show Formulas display again.
2. Get a printout of the formula display.
3. Change back to normal display.
4. Save the spreadsheet as MONEY3.

MOVING INFORMATION BETWEEN SPREADSHEETS

Sometimes you need to take information out of one spreadsheet and include it in another. In the process of moving information, the information can be copied (the original stays intact) or moved (the original is removed).

1. Create a new spreadsheet by selecting Create New File... from the File menu option.

   The spreadsheet has the temporary filename SHEET2.WKS.

2. In cell A1, enter the text **MY BUDGET.**
3. Make MONEY3.WKS active by selecting that file from the Window menu option.

   The spreadsheet MONEY3 is displayed.

4. Select rows 1 to 7.
5. Select the Copy command from the Edit menu option.

Now, you will copy the information into the spreadsheet SHEET2 at cell A2.

PRACTICE TIME

Make SHEET2 active.

You need to select the cell where the top left corner of the information should be positioned.

6. Select cell A2.
7. Press [Enter].

   The information from MONEY3 is inserted, as shown in Figure 7-6.

8. Save the spreadsheet as file MYBUDGET.

Figure 7-6

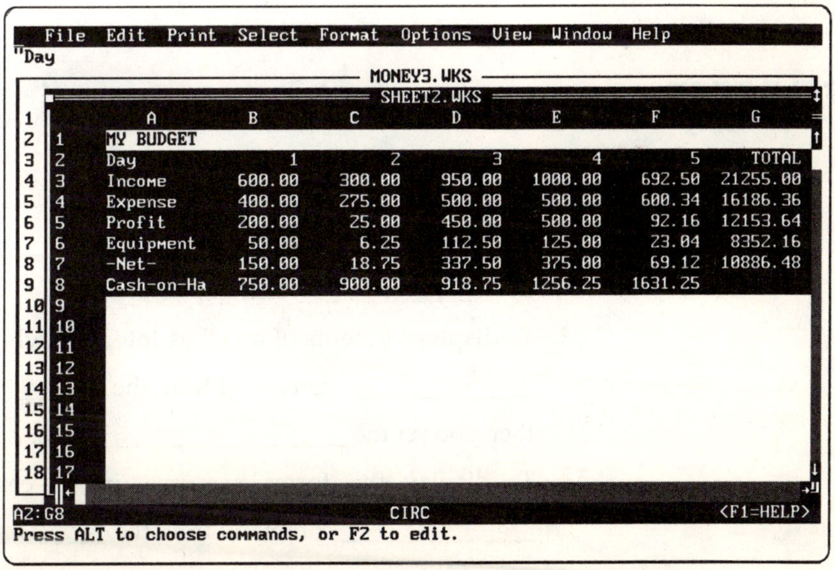

QUITTING THE SESSION

This is the end of this lesson. To quit, follow the instructions given in Lesson One. Save any changes you made to the files.

SUMMARY OF COMMANDS

Topic or Feature	*Command or Reference*	*Menu*	*Page*
Displaying bold characters	Style...	Format	72
Setting display format of numbers and other options	General, Fixed..., Dollar...	Format	74
Moving information to new cells	Select cells; then Move	Edit	75
Deleting columns	Select columns; then Delete	Edit	76
Displaying formulas	Show Formulas	Options	77
Moving data between spreadsheets	Select cells; then Move Make other spreadsheet active, position cursor, and then Enter	Edit	78

SELF-TEST

1. To select the entire spreadsheet, ______________________________.
2. To display a cell in bold, you select the ____________ command from the ____________ menu option.
3. To display contents of a cell as integers (whole numbers), you use the ____________ command from the ____________ menu option, and then you set the ________________ to 0.
4. To display the formula entries in all cells on screen, select the ____________ command from the ____________ menu option.

5. When you Move contents, the original contents ______________ (remain intact/are erased).
6. To move the contents of a cell, you select the ______________ command from the ______________ menu option.
7. To make another open file active, you select that filename from the ______________ menu.
8. When copying data from one spreadsheet to another, you select the cells to be copied, give the Move command, ______________________, and then locate the cursor where you want the data inserted.
9. To delete several consecutive columns, you ______________ the columns and then select the ______________ command from the ______________ menu option.

LESSON EIGHT

Database: Creating Files

OBJECTIVES

In this lesson you will learn how to:

- Understand database terminology.
- Create a database file.
- Specify fields to be included in a database.
- Enter information into a database file.
- Change display width and numerical format.
- Use concepts of Form and List layouts.
- Find information in a database.
- Save a database file on disk.

STARTING OFF

First, start up your computer and enter the Works program. Follow the instructions given in Lesson One so that the initial screen is displayed. Insert your data disk into a disk drive.

CREATING A DATABASE FILE

To create a database file, do the following:

1. Select the Create New File... command from the File menu option.
2. Select the <New Database> option.

   The database Form screen is displayed, as shown in Figure 8-1.

At the top of the screen is the menu bar. The default filename, DATA1.WDB, appears at the center of the top line in the work area. When you save the database, you will give it a more descriptive name.

Figure 8-1

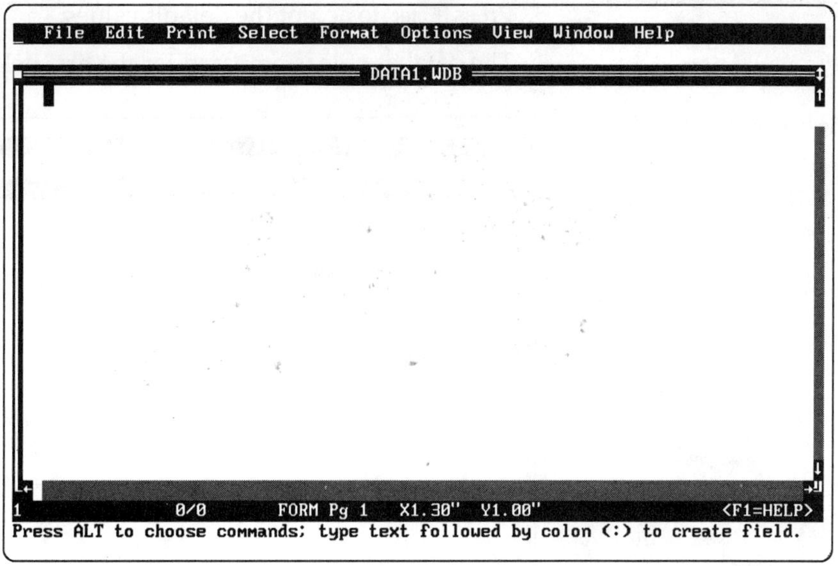

ENTERING FIELD NAMES

First you need to specify what information you want to keep in the file. For example, in a student file you might need to keep track of each student's ID number, name, address, telephone number, birthdate, and grade level. Each one of these items is a **field,** and each block of a single student's data is a **record.**

The Form screen is used to display information on a single record. It is blank now. You create fields on this screen by typing field names anywhere in the work area. Each field name must be followed by a colon (:). Field names may consist of letters, numbers, spaces, and other characters except the single quote ('). A database cannot contain two fields with identical names. After you enter a field name and colon, and press [Enter], a dialog box lets you set the field width and height. The field width and height (number of rows) should be large enough to display the data you will enter.

You are creating a file of customer records. You want to include the following fields: customer number, name, address, city, state, zip code, telephone number, credit status, and balance. You will begin by moving the highlight to the position on the screen where you want to enter the first field name.

1. Move the highlight, using the arrow keys, down and to the right until the status line displays X3.00″ Y1.50″.

2. Type **Cust #:** and press [Enter].

   A dialog box appears with default values of field width 20 and height 1.

3. Press Enter to accept the default values.

   The database file is prepared for the first field, as shown in Figure 8-2.

Figure 8-2

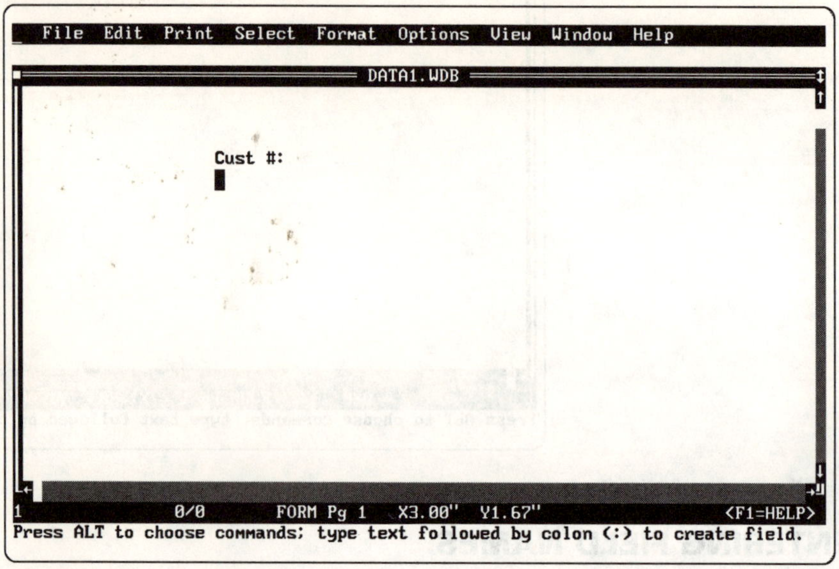

You can now enter the second field, which is "Name." Let's divide that into two fields: "First Name" and "Last Name."

4. Type **First Name:** and press Enter.
5. Press Enter to accept the dialog bow defaults.

   "First Name:" appears below "Cust #:" in the work area.

You will enter the rest of the field names in the same manner.

Correcting Errors

If you notice a typing error before you press Enter, either backspace and correct the error or press Esc to erase the entry and start again. If you notice an error afterward, don't worry about it for the time being. You will have a chance to correct it later.

PRACTICE TIME

Enter the rest of the fields, as shown here. Where indicated, change the field width from the default value to the number indicated. To do so, type that number in the appropriate space in the dialog box.

Last Name:
Address:
City:
State: (change field width to 2)
ZIP: (change field width to 5)
Telephone: (change field width to 14)
Credit Status:
Balance: (change field width to 8)

Numeric Format

Numbers entered into a field can be displayed several ways, like in a spreadsheet. The Balance field, for example, should always display two digits to the right of the decimal point. You can select the format used to display this field.

1. Move the highlight up one row and to the right once so that "Balance" is displayed at the left of the status bar beneath the work area and the eight-space field for displaying data is highlighted.

2. Select the Fixed... command in the Format menu.

   A dialog is displayed for setting the number of decimals.

3. Press [Enter] to accept the default value, 2.

ENTERING RECORDS

The Form screen, where you initially entered the field names, is also used to enter data into the database file. To the left of the word FORM on the status line is displayed "0/0," which means there are no records of data in the file. Generally, the two numbers indicate the number of records displayed and the total number of records in the file. You will now enter data into the file.

The line below the menu bar is the **entry bar.** It is initially blank. It works like in the spreadsheet. You make an entry into a field by selecting the field and typing the data. As you type the data, it appears on the entry bar. If you notice an error, you can press [Backspace] to back up and make corrections, or [Esc] to erase the entry. When you finish typing the entry, you should visually verify the entry as displayed on the entry bar before pressing [Enter] or another keystroke to complete the entry.

Suppose that your first customer is **Sam Sherman,** who lives at **3983 West Blvd., Los Angeles, CA 90016.** His telephone number is **(213) 295-9443,** and his credit rating is **Preferred.** His customer number is **29364,** and his current balance is **356.74.**

You need to move the cursor to the data area for the first field.

1. Move the highlight two spaces to the right of Cust #:.

   The data field for the customer number is highlighted, as shown in Figure 8-3.

Figure 8-3

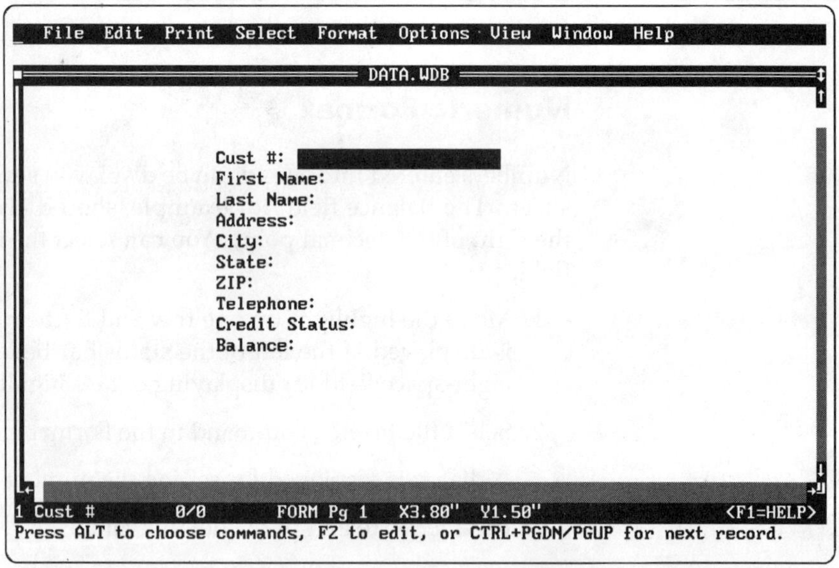

2. Type **29364** and press Enter.

   What you type appears on the entry bar and in the data area for the field, as shown in Figure 8-4.

3. Select the First Name data field by pressing Tab.

4. Type **Sam** and press Tab.

   The name "Sam" appears next to First Name and the next data area is highlighted.

Are you beginning to get the idea? You select the data field, type your entry, and then press Enter or Tab. Both keystrokes complete your entry, but Tab also moves the highlight to the next data field.

Figure 8-4

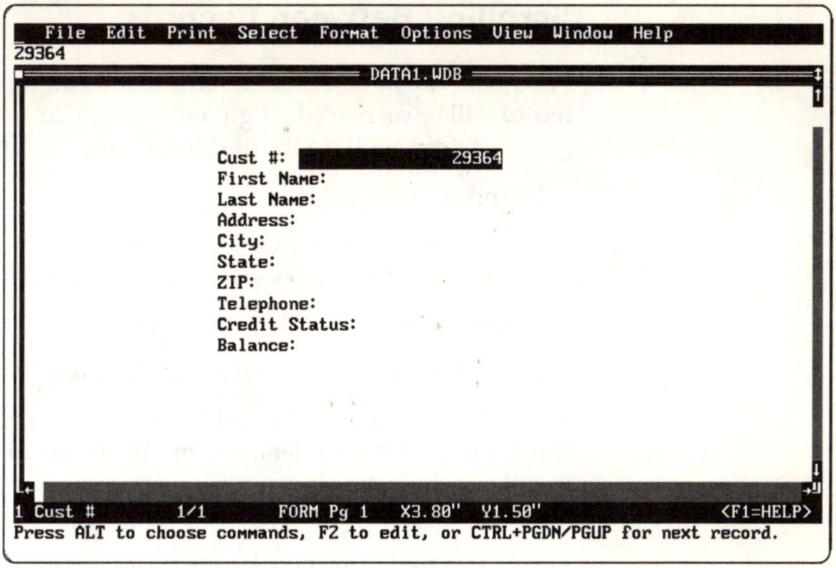

PRACTICE TIME

Make entries for the rest of the fields. Don't worry if a line by the field name isn't long enough to display all your entry. After you type the entry for Balance, press Enter. When you are done, your screen should look like Figure 8-5.

Figure 8-5

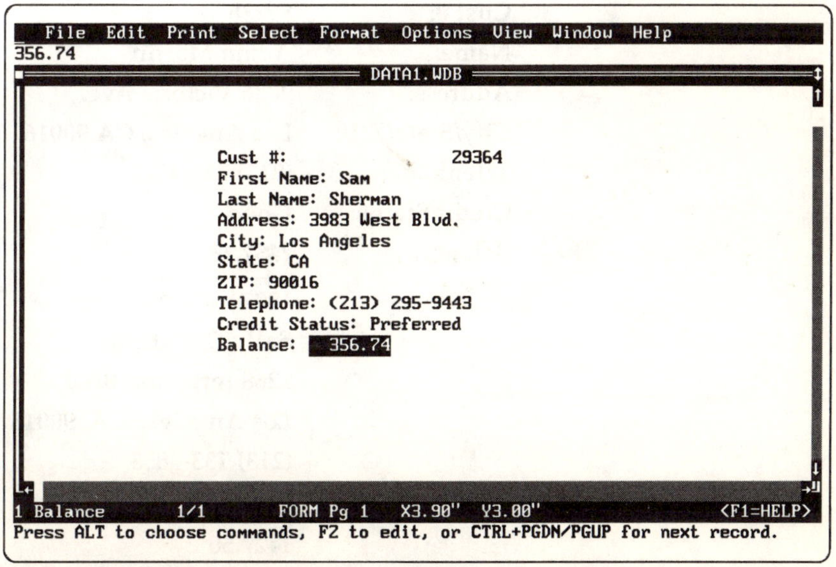

Scrolling Between Records

When you finish filling out a record, you could press Tab and a new, blank record will be displayed. Right now, since you completed the last entry with Enter, you can **scroll** to the next form using Ctrl-Pg Dn.

1. Press Ctrl-Pg Dn.

   A blank form is displayed; the number 2 at the extreme left of the status line indicates you are on the second record in the file.

2. If necessary, select the Cust # field.

Note: Ctrl-Pg Up *scrolls to the previous record.*

You will enter data and scroll to the next record over and over until you exhaust your customer data. When a blank record is displayed after you have completed the last customer record, you will press Esc. Make sure to visually check your entry for each field before going on to the next field.

- If you find a mistake before you complete an entry, either erase what you've typed using Backspace or press Esc and retype the entry.
- If you notice an error on an earlier entry, select the field, press Delete, and then enter the correct data.

PRACTICE TIME

Fill out nine more records using the following information. If no credit status is indicated, leave the field blank. Stop when a blank record is displayed after you have entered the information for the last customer.

Cust #:	**89238**
Name:	**Adam Martin**
Address:	**2836 Victoria Ave.**
City/State/ZIP:	**Los Angeles, CA 90016**
Telephone:	**(213) 747-4221**
Credit Status:	**Good**
Balance:	**2437.18**
	19274
	Sally Davidson
	1268 Jefferson Blvd.
	Los Angeles, CA 90018
	(213) 733 1855
	Preferred
	1427.50
	18392

Alex Johnson

8293 Cypress Road

Reno, NV 89503

(702) 748-9112

Good

892.00

84938

Bill Barth

9177 Honeywell Dr.

Reno, NV 89512

(702) 323-3633

400.25

97021

Jackie Swain

11836 Power Street

Sparks, NV 89431

(702) 359-4223

Preferred

3400.50

54896

Kathy Starbird

1124 Atlantic Street

Albany, CA 94706

(415) 839-4886

Good

1237.00

82394

William Peterson

3414 Indiana Ave.

San Jose, CA 95100

(408) 299-2037

Good

5060.17

47740

Larry Duncan
9051 Star Court
Downey, CA 90240
(213) 927-9727
69.00

83333
Richard Bateman
3740 San Augustin Dr.
Anaheim, CA 92800
(714) 363-4851
Good
457.25

SAVING YOUR WORK

The database file that you created is in the computer's random access memory. If you turn off the computer, you lose that information. To keep it for future use, you must save your database file on a disk. You will use the name CUSTOMER to save the database file on the data disk.

1. Select the Save As... command from the File menu option.

   A dialog box appears.

2. Make sure the drive with your data disk is selected.
3. Enter **CUSTOMER** in the filename box.

   Works saves the database file and returns to the database screen.

THE LIST AND FORM LAYOUTS

Records (and the information) in the database can be displayed in one of two layouts: **form** or **list**. When you entered data, the form layout was displayed. The form layout displays records one at a time. All the fields and their contents are listed, one field per line, on the screen. You can easily switch the display to the list layout.

1. Select the List command from the View menu option.
2. Press [Pg Up] to move to the beginning of the data.

   The screen should look similar to Figure 8-6.

The list layout can display up to 18 records at a time. Not all the fields can be displayed at any one time. Each record is displayed horizontally, with the appropriate information beneath the field name at the top of each column. Right now, the first 7 fields are displayed for all 10 records. You can view other fields by pressing the left- and right-arrow keys.

Each field initially displays 10 characters of data, independent of the field widths entered for the form layout. You will change the widths of some of these columns in a little while.

You can use the list layout to view all the records in the file. Because you only have 10 records in the file, you can see all the records on one screen. When there are more records than can be shown on one screen, you can vertically scroll the screen to see other records.

Figure 8-6

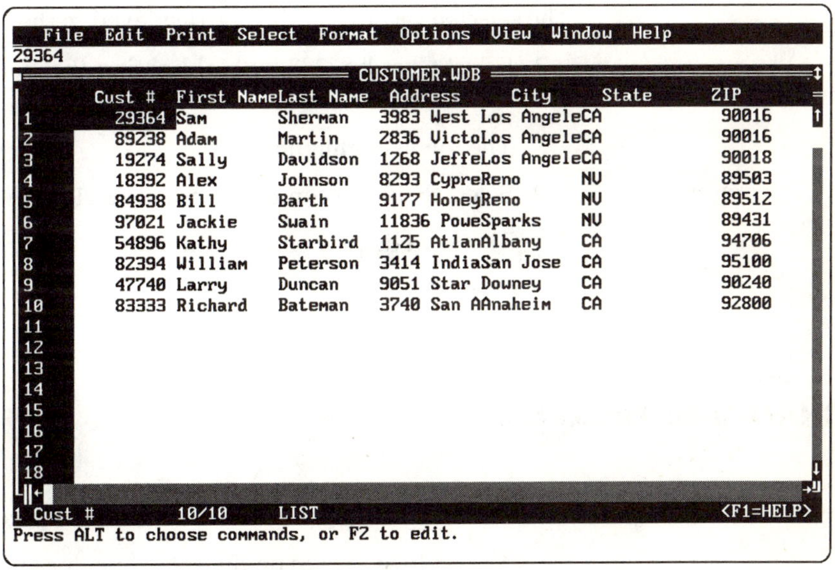

CHANGING THE FIELD DISPLAY WIDTH

The data in the address field is wider than the screen display. You can change the display width so that the whole entry can be seen.

1. Use the mouse or arrow keys to highlight the address field in any record.
2. Select the Field Width... command from the Format menu option.

   A dialog box appears with the default width of 10.
3. Change the width to **22.**

   The list layout displays all the address data.

The field display widths are set independently in the list and form layouts. You will change the display width of the address field in the form layout so it displays all the information in the last record.

SELECTING A RECORD

You can select any record by using the Record command in the Select menu. The selected record can then be displayed in the form layout.

1. Select Cust # 83333 by highlighting that cell and selecting the Record command in the Select menu option.

   The row is highlighted.
2. Select the Form command from the View menu option.

   The form displays information on customer number 83333.

CHANGING FIELD SIZE

1. Press [Tab] until the address field is highlighted.

   The address shown on the entry line does not fit into the specified field width.
2. Select the Field Size... command from the Format menu option.
3. Change the width to **22.**

   The data are now displayed for the field.
4. Return to the list layout.
5. Adjust the display so all records appear on the screen.

FINDING INFORMATION

Before ending this lesson, let's briefly see how information can be retrieved quickly. This is accomplished by using the Search command from the Select menu option.

1. Highlight a cell beneath the data, say in row 12.
2. Select the Search... command from the Select menu option.

   A dialog box appears.
3. In the Search for box, enter **90016** (do not press Enter).
4. Select the All Records option in the Match box.
5. Select the <OK> button.

   Only two records are displayed. Both have ZIP codes that match the search condition.
6. Select the Show All Records command from the Select menu option to display all records on the screen again.

You can use the Search command to find names or numbers. Text searches are not case-sensitive. That is, the search ignores whether information is in uppercase or lowercase letters.

UPDATING (EDITING) THE DATA

You might select a record to be displayed because you need to change or update information in it. Or, after looking at a record, you might find a mistake that should be corrected. In either case, you need to change (edit) the data for a field.

To change an entry, you select the cell that contains the entry and retype the entry. The new entry replaces the old one. For example, suppose Sally Davidson changes her name to Sally Brown. You will update her record.

1. Make sure you are in the list layout.
2. Select the cell that contains Davidson. (You may want to try the Search command.)
3. Type **Brown** and press Enter.

PRINTING THE DATABASE

To print out the database, you use the Print menu, much as you did for the word processor or spreadsheet.

1. Select the Print... command from the Print menu option.

   A dialog box appears.

2. Select the <Print> command option.

   All the records are printed, taking two pages.

You can also print the data for a single record. To do so, you need to be in the form layout.

1. Change the display to the form layout.
2. Select the Print... command from the Print menu.

   A dialog box appears. At the right there is a box indicating which records will be printed.

3. Verify that only the current record will be printed.
4. Select the <Print> button.

   The printout of one record looks like the form layout.

QUITTING THE SESSION

This is the end of this lesson. Follow the instructions given in Lesson One to quit. Make sure you save the changes to your database file.

SUMMARY OF COMMANDS

Topic or Feature	*Command or Reference*	*Menu*	*Page*
Adjusting the width of a field (form or list layout)	Field Width...	Format	91
Changing the display format of a numeric field	General, Fixed..., and other formats	Format	85
Saving a file	Save or Save As...	File	90
Display in form layout	Form	View	90

Display in list layout	List	View	90
Finding information	Search...	Select	93
Displaying only records that meet a condition	Search... All records option	Select	93
Displaying all records	Show All Records	Select	93
Printing the database	Print... from the list layout	Print	94
Printing one record	Print... from the form layout	Print	94

■ SELF-TEST

1. In an inventory database, the purchase date, item description, quantity, and value may be separate ______________ in the ______________.
2. The numeric display format is changed by using a command from the ______________ menu.
3. If an entry is too long for the default width of a field, the entered data is ______________ (lost/still kept in memory).
4. When you complete an entry by pressing __________, the entry is made and the field below is selected.
5. When entering field names, always end the name with a ____________.
6. On a __________ layout, each record appears horizontally in one row with the appropriate information beneath the field names at the top of each column.
7. To change the field display width, you select the field and then select the ______________ command from the ______________ menu.
8. To change the entry for a field, you select the field and then ______________________________.
9. To find the record containing certain text, select the __________ command from the __________ menu option.
10. To print the database, select the ______________ command from the ______________ menu option.

LESSON NINE

Database: Manipulating the Data

OBJECTIVES

In this lesson you will learn how to:

- Arrange (sort) records in a database file.
- Select records based on single, multiple, and numeric conditions.
- Update (change) information in existing records.
- Change the display format of the list layout.
- Insert records in an existing database file.
- Copy records within a database file.
- Delete records in a database file.
- Save file to disk using the same filename.

STARTING OFF

Start up your computer and enter the Works program so that the initial screen is displayed. Insert your data disk from Lesson Eight into a disk drive.

First you will retrieve the database file from the last lesson.

1. Select the Open Existing File... command from the File menu option.
2. Select the drive that contains your data disk, and select the <OK> button.
3. In the Files box, select the Database file CUSTOMER.WDB and press the <OK> button.

   The form layout for CUSTOMER is displayed, as shown in Figure 9-1.

PRACTICE TIME

Display the form for customer number 82394, William Peterson. Do not use the Search command.

Figure 9-1

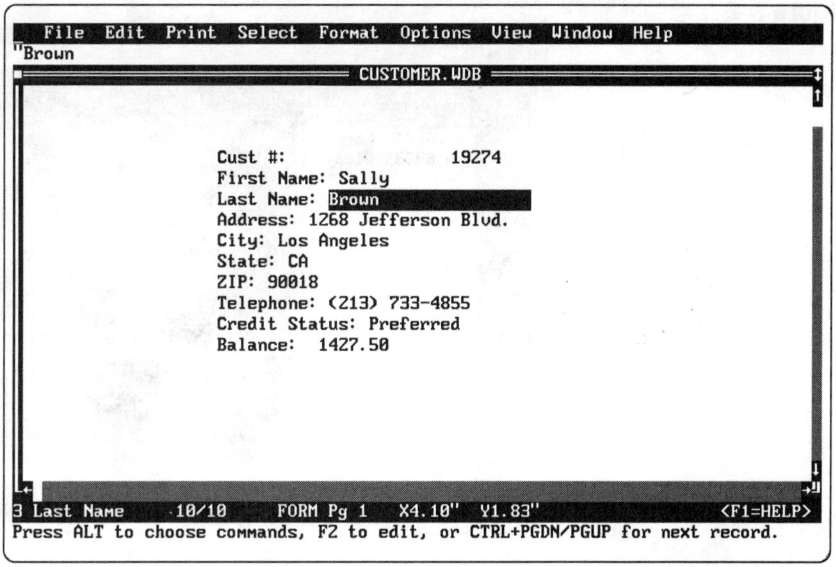

How did you do? Although this file does not contain very many records, it may have taken awhile to find customer number 82394 by using Ctrl-Pg Up and Ctrl-Pg Dn to scroll through the file because the records are not arranged in any specific order. What if there were 1,000 records? Then, even in the list layout, you might have to scroll through many screens. If the display were organized by customer number, it would not be as difficult.

ARRANGING RECORDS

Works lets you arrange the records in a file in whatever order you want. Records can be arranged in alphabetical order (A to Z or Z to A) or in numerical order (ascending or descending) for any category you select.

Let's rearrange the records so they are in ascending numerical order by customer number. This is done using the Sort command.

1. Position the highlight on the Cust # data field.
2. Return to the list layout.
3. Select the Sort Records... command from the Select menu option.

   A dialog box is displayed, as shown in Figure 9-2.

4. Make sure the first field is Cust # and is ascending.
5. Select the <OK> button.

Figure 9-2

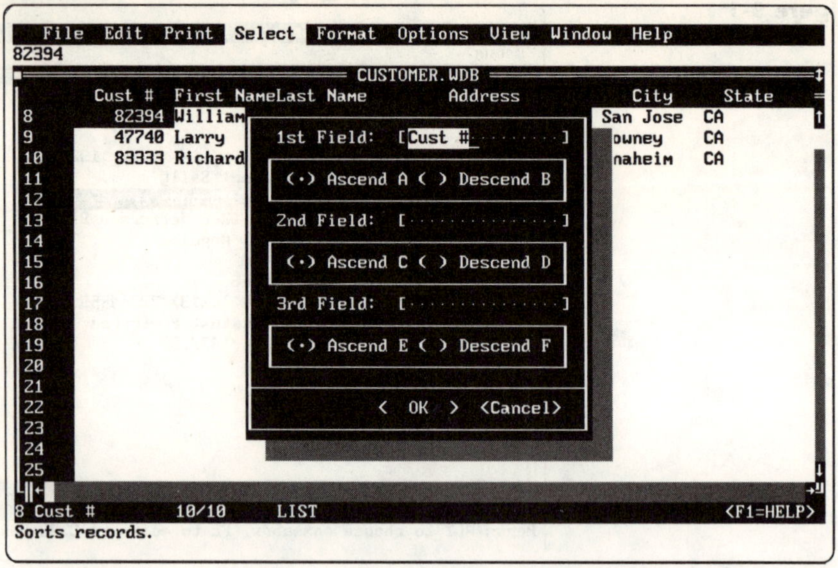

The records are now arranged in customer number order.

That was fast, wasn't it? Now you will rearrange the file in alphabetical order by last names.

6. Select the Sort Records... command from the Select menu option.
7. Change the first sort field by typing **Last Name,** and make sure it is ascending.
8. Select the <OK> command option.

   The records are arranged alphabetically by last name.

You can sort from the form layout, too. You can try this on your own.

PRACTICE TIME

Put the records back in ascending numerical order by customer number.

SELECTING RECORDS

The Search command is useful for locating records that contain a certain value (or entry). However, you cannot specify the field in which that value is to appear. For example, if you are looking for a record that contains the text "star," Works will locate both the record for "Kathy Starbird" and the one for Larry Duncan, who lives on "Star Court." You can be more specific by defining and using a **query.**

1. Select the Query command from the View menu option.

   The Query screen appears. It looks like the Form screen.

You enter the conditions for selecting records in the Query screen. Conditions may include text matches, numerical values or ranges, or dates. Conditions are entered in the data fields and begin with an operator, usually = (equals sign). Text matches are entered within quotation marks, and date matches are entered within apostrophes. Conditions may use the * wildcard, as in DOS commands. These will be explained as examples require their use.

For example, to search for all records with the last name "Starbird," you would enter **="Starbird"** in the data field for Last Name. Suppose you want to find all records with telephone numbers in area code 702. That is, the field begins with (702) and anything may follow. The * wildcard lets the condition accept all telephone numbers in the area code.

2. Press [Tab] to select the Telephone data field and then enter **="(702)*"**.

3. Press [F10] to exit the Query screen.

   Three records appear on the list screen, as shown in Figure 9-3. All three have telephone numbers in area code 702.

Figure 9-3

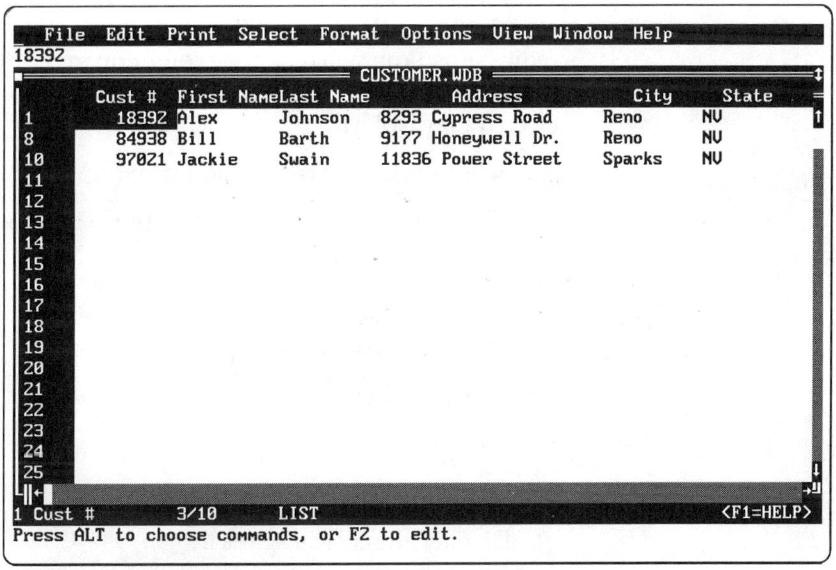

Only the records that match the query conditions are displayed in the list or form screens, which is useful if you want to print information using only those selected records. When done, you can again display all the records in the database.

4. Select the Show All Records command from the Select menu option to list all records.

In addition to the = operator, conditions may begin with > (greater than), < (less than), >= (greater than or equal to), <= (less than or equal to), and <> (not equal to).

PRACTICE TIME

Perform searches for each of the following cases. To clear an earlier condition, select that field and enter a blank.

1. The Credit Status field contains an entry (>"").
2. The Balance greater than 1000 (>1000).
3. Display all records.

MULTIPLE SELECTION CONDITIONS

You can use more than one condition for record selection. For example, you can select records of customers who live in Nevada (NV) and have Good credit status. You will enter one condition in the State field and another in the Credit Status field. Only those records that meet both conditions will be selected for display.

1. Select the Query command from the View menu option.
2. Clear the previous criterion by replacing it with a blank.
3. Select State and enter **="NV"**.

   The field width is too narrow to display all the entry, but the entry line above the work area displays the condition.
4. Select Credit Status and enter **="Good"**.
5. Press F10.

   One record (for Alex Johnson) is selected.
6. Display all records again.

NUMERIC RANGE SELECTION

Sometimes you need to select records that contain values that are within a certain numeric range, such as to find all the customers whose balance is between $1,000 and $2,000. In a condition, the symbols &, |, and ~ represent the AND, OR, and NOT operators, respectively.

1. Select the Query command from the View menu option.
2. Clear the previous conditions.
3. Select Balance and enter **>1000&<2000.**

The & indicates that the two conditions for Balance must both be satisfied (AND operator).

4. Press F10 to view the records that meet the conditions.

   Two records meet the conditions.

5. Display all records again.

If you want to select records that meet either of two conditions, like Credit Status of Preferred *or* Balance greater than 1000, the conditions need to be entered in one field. (Entering these conditions in their respective fields is interpreted as AND.) To do so, in *any* field you could enter **=(Credit Status="Preferred") | (Balance>1000)** as the condition. The field name is required before the operator for that field's condition.

PRACTICE TIME

Try changing the record selection conditions.

1. Select all customers whose credit status is Preferred or whose balance is more than $1,000.00.
2. Select all customers whose ZIP is in the range 90000 to 90050.
3. Select all customers whose last names do not begin with B (<>"B*").
4. Select all customers whose ZIP is not within the range 90000 to 99999.
5. Display all records again.

CHANGING FIELD DISPLAY ORDER

You can change the order in which fields appear in the list layout. Because the first six fields are displayed, changing the order may change which fields are displayed.

Suppose you decide that it would be more useful if the credit status and balance are displayed in the list layout instead of the address and city. You want to move Credit Status and Balance (which are the last two fields in the record) to the fourth and fifth positions, respectively.

1. In the list layout, highlight the Balance field of any record.
2. Select the Field command in the Select menu option.
3. Select the Move command in the Edit menu option.

   The message line instructs you to select the new location.
4. Highlight the Address field of any record.
5. Press [Enter].

   The Balance field is relocated before the Address field.

PRACTICE TIME

1. Move the Credit Status field to the fourth field in the display.
2. Move the Credit Status and Balance fields back where they were—that is, make them the last two fields in the display.

INSERTING A RECORD

You just got a new customer. He is to be customer number **69248.** His name is **Bruce Morrison,** and he lives at **2080 Guatemala Street, Beaverton, OR 97005.** His telephone number is **(503) 646-6892.** He does not have a credit status yet, and his balance is **$125.00.** You would like to insert his record in the file so that the file is still in ascending numerical order by customer number. This could be done by adding the record to the end of the file and sorting again by customer number. But right now, you will insert the record at its proper place in sequence from the list layout.

1. Make sure that you are in the list layout and that the records are in ascending numerical order by customer number.

Customer number 69248 should go between customer numbers 54896 and 82394. New records are always inserted immediately before the record the cursor is on when you enter the insert mode. In this case, you want to select customer number 82394.

2. Highlight customer number 82394.
3. Select the Insert Record/Field command from the Edit menu option.

   A dialog box appears.

You want to insert a record.

4. Select Record and then select the <OK> button.

   A blank record appears between customer numbers 54896 and 82394.

5. Select the Form command from the View menu option.
6. Enter the information for all fields.
7. Select the List command from the View menu option.

NOTE: You can insert a new record from the form layout too. When you select the Insert command, the new record is inserted immediately before the record that was displayed.

COPYING RECORDS

In creating (inserting) new records, if some of the new entries are the same as in an existing record, you can copy these. You can copy an entire record or just some fields.

William Peterson's wife, Joan, is a new customer. You will copy the last name, address, and telephone number from William Peterson's record. The new customer number is 32097. Her balance is 247.09 and she does not have a credit status yet. Also, this time you will add the record to the end of the file and then sort on customer number.

William Peterson's customer number is 82394.

1. Select William Peterson's record. This is done by highlighting a cell in the record and then selecting the Record command from the Select menu option.
2. Select the Copy command from the Edit menu option.
3. Highlight a cell in the first blank row beneath the data.
4. Press Enter.

   The data in the selected record is copied to the new record.

5. Select the Form command from the View menu option.

   Now you need to fill in the rest of the information.

PRACTICE TIME

1. Edit the copy of William Peterson's record so that the customer number is **32097** and the first name is **Joan**. Also, credit status should be blanked and balance changed to **247.09.**
2. Sort the records in ascending order by customer number.

DELETING A RECORD

Now that you know how to insert a record, let's delete a record. You will delete the record for Richard Bateman. Again, this can be done using either the list or form layout. The command deletes the selected record.

1. Make sure that you are in the list layout.
2. Highlight any cell in the record for Richard Bateman. His customer number is 83333.
3. Select the Record command from the Select menu option.
4. Select the Delete Record/Field command from the Edit menu option.

   The record for Richard Bateman is deleted.

You can delete consecutive records by selecting several records and then issuing the Delete command. If you want to delete all the records that meet specific conditions, but are not necessarily consecutive records in the file, use the query command so that only those records are displayed on the screen. Then, select them all and delete them. You may try this feature on your own.

SAVING THE DATABASE AGAIN

You have made quite a few changes to the database. These changes were made only to the database in the main memory of your computer. The disk file for CUSTOMER has not been changed. If you turn off the computer, all the changes you made in this lesson will be lost.

PRACTICE TIME

Save the file as CUSTOMR1.

QUITTING THE SESSION

This is the end of this lesson. Follow the instructions given in Lesson One to quit.

SUMMARY OF COMMANDS

Topic or Feature	*Command or Reference*	*Menu*	*Page*
Sorting records	Sort Records...	Select	97
Selecting records	Record	Select	98
Selecting fields	Field	Select	98
Viewing list layout	List	View	99
Viewing form layout	Form	View	99
Entering multiple selection conditions	Query	View	100
Performing a query	F10		99
Changing field order in list layout	Select the field, then Move, then locate new field position and press Enter	Edit	102
Inserting a record	Select place in file, then Insert Record/Field	Edit	102
Copying a record	Select the record to be copied, then Copy then locate new record position and press Enter	Edit	103
Deleting a record	Select the record, then Delete Record/Field	Edit	104

SELF-TEST

1. To arrange the database file in order by a specific field, select the ____________ command in the ____________ menu option.

2. Changes made to the format in the form layout ___________ (do/do not) affect the format of the list layout.
3. To specify a selection condition, select the ______________ command from the ___________ menu option.
4. When you enter selection conditions in two different fields, they are equivalent to the ___________ (AND/OR) operator.
5. The selection conditions for all records with balance between 100 and 200 might read: ______________________________________.
6. To change the order fields are displayed in the list layout, you do the following: ______________________________________.
7. When a new record is inserted in the middle of a file, it is inserted ___________ (before/after) the selected record.
8. To copy information from one record to another, you first ______________________________________; then you ____________________.
9. To delete a record from a database file, you use the ___________ command in the ___________ menu option.
10. To delete all records that meet a specific set of conditions but that are not consecutive in the display, you first ______________________________.

LESSON TEN

Database: Printing Reports and Changing Structure

OBJECTIVES

In this lesson you will learn how to:

- Understand the concept of report format.
- Define a report format.
- Define a report format with selected records.
- Define a report format with selected fields.
- Change the database structure.

STARTING OFF

Start your computer and enter the Works program so that the initial screen is displayed. Place your data disk from Lesson Nine into a disk drive.

First you will retrieve the database file you worked on in the last lesson.

1. Select the Open Existing File... command from the File menu option.
2. Select the drive containing your data disk and then select the <OK> button.
3. Select file CUSTOMR1.WDB in the Files box and then select the <OK> button.

   The database from the last lesson appears in list layout.

DEFINING A REPORT

In Lesson Eight, you printed information as it appeared in the list and form layouts. You can also print the data as a **report,** which contains data arranged in report columns with headings. You specify the contents and format by

defining a report. Here, you will create a customer listing report. The first report you create will list all fields for all customers.

Before you define the report, you should adjust the column widths in the list layout to eliminate all unnecessary spaces. This is not required, but you should do it first so you don't have to adjust the column widths within the report definition.

PRACTICE TIME

Use the Field Width... command from the Format menu option to adjust the widths of the fields so all data are displayed and unnecessary spaces are eliminated.

---

1. Select the New Report command from the View menu option.

   A screen similar to Figure 10-1 is displayed.

Figure 10-1

```
_






Cust #First NaLast NameAddress            City        Sta

18392 Alex     Johnson  8293 Cypress Road    Reno        NV
19274 Sally    Brown    1268 Jefferson Blvd. Los Angeles CA
29364 Sam      Sherman  3983 West Blvd.      Los Angeles CA
32097 Joan     Peterson 3414 Indiana Ave.    San Jose    CA
47740 Larry    Duncan   9051 Star Court      Downey      CA
54896 Kathy    Starbird 1125 Atlantic Street Albany      CA
69248 Bruce    Morrison 2080 Guatemala Street Beaverton  OR
82394 William  Peterson 3414 Indiana Ave.    San Jose    CA
84938 Bill     Barth    9177 Honeywell Dr.   Reno        NV
89238 Adam     Martin   2836 Victoria Ave.   Los Angeles CA
97021 Jackie   Swain    11836 Power Street   Sparks      NV


Page 1                    REPORT
Press ENTER to continue, ESC to cancel.
```

   This screen is a preview of what the top part of the first page of your report will look like when printed. The New Report command generates default specifications for the report consisting of all the fields, of widths specified for the list layout.

2. Press [Enter] four times to view both preview pages of the report.

   After that, the Report screen appears, as shown in Figure 10-2.

Figure 10-2

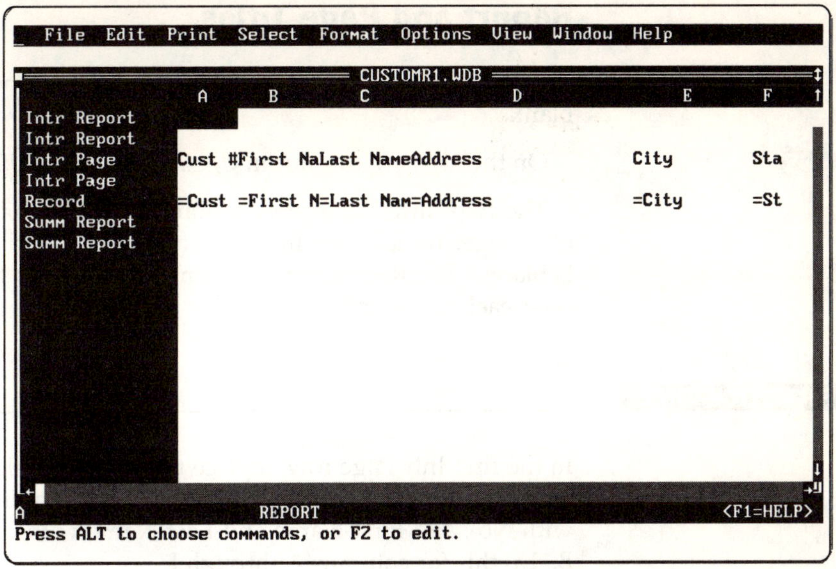

You use the report screen to specify what information is to be included in the report. The report screen resembles a spreadsheet screen, with **report columns,** labeled A, B, C, and so on, across the top margin and **row types,** named Intr Report, Intr Page, and so on, down the left margin. The row type defines how the information in that row is laid out in the report. The row types initially shown on the report screen are used as follows:

Intr Report	The contents of the Intr Report rows are printed at the top of the first page of the report and serve as a title for the report.
Intr Page	The contents of the Intr Page rows serve as column labels for the report. They are printed at the top of the report columns on each page of the report. The initial contents of the first Intr Page row are the field names, truncated according to the field widths in the list layout.
Record	The contents of the Record row are used to make up the body of the report. The Record row generates one line in the report for each record displayed in the list layout. Initially, each report column contains the contents of one field in the database.
Summ Report	The Summ Report rows are printed at the end of the report. This row type may be used for column totals or for text.

You can enter text, numbers, dates, or formulas into any column in any row type in the report screen. The text, numbers, and dates are used to identify the report, label the rows and indicate the summary information.

Report and Page Titles

The Intr Report rows are used to specify the report title. Initially they are blank.

On the top row, in column C, enter the title **CUSTOMER LISTING.**

The two Intro Page rows contain headings that are printed at the top of each page. Initially, the first row contains the field names and the second row is blank. The Record row contains formulas for the report columns. Right now, each report column contains the contents of a single field.

PRACTICE TIME

In the first Intr Page row, replace the existing field names with titles that fit within the column width limitations. For example, you could replace Cust # with No., and First Name and Last Name with Customer Name in column B. Do this for columns A through J.

Displaying Database Information

The Record row type is initially set up to print the contents of all the fields in the database. In a later example, you will manipulate the columns of the report.

Displaying Column Summaries

The Summ Report row type can be used to display column statistics. Reports can display sums, averages, maximum and minimum values, counts of the number of items (rows with data), standard deviations and variances.

You would like to sum the balances. First, you need to make sure the report can display the data. Right now, if your field width for Balance (column J) is less than 9, the report will print #'s instead of the total because the total is larger than +9999.99. You will change the column width, selecting only the Balance column. If you change the column width without selecting a column, the widths of all columns in the report will be changed.

1. Position the highlight in column J of the first Summ Report row.
2. Select the Column command from the Select menu option.
3. Select the Column Width... command from the Format menu option.
4. Change the width to 9 if it is less than 9.

5. Position the highlight at the first Summ Report row in column J.
6. Enter **=SUM(Balance)** in the cell.
7. Move the highlight to column I of the first Summ Report row.
8. Enter the label **TOTAL.**

The SUM function displays the total of all the values in the field contained between the parentheses, in this case all the values of Balance that are printed. The on-screen help describes other functions available in reports.

Specifying Page Layout

When you are generating a report, it is often helpful to preview the printout. The Preview... command gives a graphical screen display of what the printout will look like. It saves time and paper when you want to try various things.

1. Select the Preview... command from the Print menu.

   A dialog box appears.

2. Select the <Preview> button.

   The screen displays the first page of the printout, as shown in Figure 10-3.

3. Press [Pg Dn].

   The second page of the printout is displayed.

4. Press [Esc].

   The report screen reappears.

The report takes two pages because of the large number of characters displayed on each line in the Record row type. You would like the report to fit onto a single page, if possible. There are four things you can do to help make it fit:

- If any fields are wider than they need to be, change those field widths.
- If you have a wide carriage printer, specify a wider page width.
- Change the left and right margins on the page to get more print space.
- Change the size of the font.

You already optimized the field widths, so next you will work with the page setup and margins.

1. Select the Page Setup & Margins... command in the Print menu.

   A dialog box appears.

   The left and right margins are 1.3 and 1.2 inches, respectively.

Figure 10-3

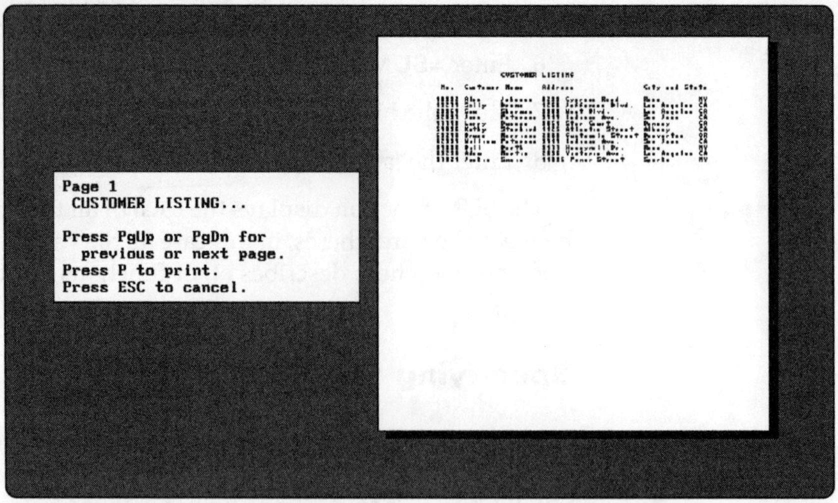

Note: If you have a wide carriage printer, you can specify 11- or 17-inch page width in the dialog box. However, Works does not easily print landscape or sideways on paper.

2. Use Tab to highlight the left margin box and type **1.0.**
3. Use Tab to highlight the right margin box and type **1.0.**
4. Select the <OK> button.

   You return to the report screen.
5. Preview the report again.

   If you do not have a wide carriage printer, the report still requires two pages.
6. Press Esc to return to the report screen.

Setting the Report Font

You can print more characters on each line if you use a smaller **font.** A font consists of two parts, a typeface and a size. The typeface (such as Courier or Helvetica) defines the shapes of the characters. The size is given in 72-ths of an inch height, called points. Twelve-point fonts print about 10 characters to an inch; fonts of smaller sizes (10-point or less) print more characters per inch. Fonts are set in the Format menu.

1. Select the Font... command in the Format menu.

   A dialog box appears with several fonts. The Sizes box displays the sizes (in points) available for the highlighted typeface.

A 7- or 8-point font is necessary to print the report on one 8 1/2-inch-wide page.

2. Highlight the various typefaces available, until one displays a font size of 8.
3. Press Tab to move the cursor to the Sizes box and highlight the 8-point size.
4. Press the <OK> button to select that font for the report.
5. Preview the report on screen to verify that it fits on one page.

Printing Date and Page Numbers

Page numbers and the current date can be printed in headers and footers on each page of the report.

1. Select the Headers & Footers... command from the Print menu.

   A dialog box appears for you to specify the header and footer contents.

Several codes are used in headers and footers, including the following:

&L	Align the following characters with the left margin.
&C	Center the following characters.
&R	Align the following characters with the right margin.
&D	Print the current date.
&P	Print the page number.

To print the date left aligned and the page number right aligned, you enter the code **&L&D&R&P** in the Header box.

2. Enter **&L&D&R&P** in the Header box.
3. Select the <OK> button.

PRINTING A REPORT

You have defined the report. Now you can print it.

1. Select the Print... command from the Print menu.

   A dialog box appears on screen.

2. Select the <OK> button.

   The report is printed.

You return to the report screen.

This section covered the techniques for specifying a report. You can experiment on your own with labels to make the report look better.

3. Select the List option in the View menu.

   You return to the list layout.

SAVING A REPORT

When you close the report-defining screen, the report becomes part of the database. You can name the report for later identification.

1. Select the Reports... command from the View menu.

   A dialog box appears on the screen, as shown in Figure 10-4.

Figure 10-4

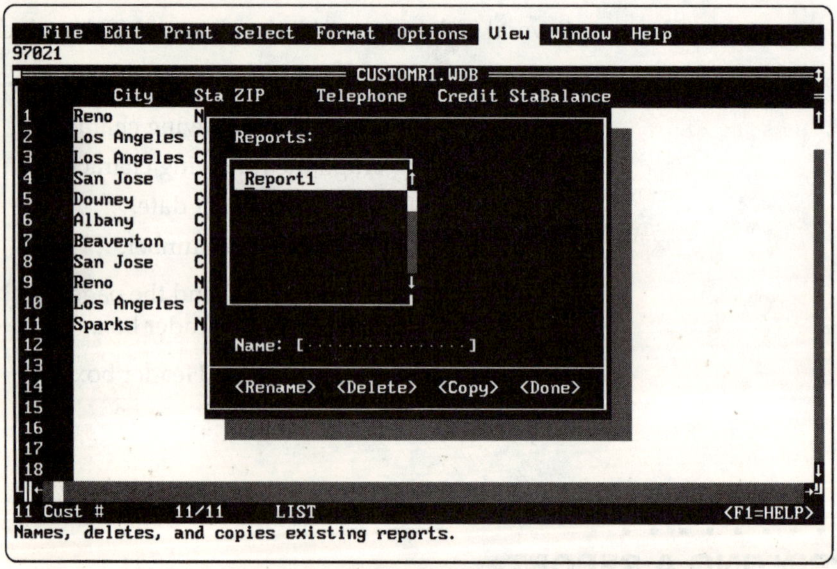

Report1, the default name of the report, is highlighted in the Reports box. You want to change the report name to Customer.

2. Press Tab to move the highlight to the Name box.
3. Type **Customer** (do not press Enter).
4. Select the <Rename> button.

The report is renamed.

5. Select the <Done> button to return to the Report screen. You return to the list layout.

DISPLAYING SELECTED RECORDS IN A REPORT

You will now use the CUSTOMER report to display only selected records.

PRACTICE TIME

Display in the list layout the records of all customers who live in California.

---

1. Select the 1 Customer command from the View menu option.

   The report is displayed on screen. Only the records displayed in the list layout are contained in the report.

2. Press [Esc].

   The report screen is displayed.

PRACTICE TIME

1. Print the report.
2. Return to the list layout.

DISPLAYING SELECTED FIELDS IN A REPORT

Sometimes you may want a report that displays only certain fields and then perhaps in a different order than they appear in the database. For example, suppose you want a report that contains the customer's last name, first name, and balance. To do this, you move those fields you want displayed to the correct order and you delete the other fields (columns). You have done most of the report setup already. You can copy the existing report specification and work on the copy.

1. Select 1 CUSTOMER in the View menu.
2. Place the highlight on column D, containing the Address field.
3. Select columns D through I either by using the mouse (holding down the left button while you extend the highlight by moving the mouse) or the keyboard (holding down Shift while using the arrow keys to extend the highlight).
4. Select the Delete Row/Column command from the Edit menu.

   A dialog box appears. You must select whether to delete the selected row or the selected columns.
5. Select the Column option and press the <OK> button.

   You return to the report screen. The selected columns were deleted.

Next you need to delete column A, which contains the customer numbers.

6. Move the highlight to a cell in column A.
7. Select the Delete Row/Column command in the Edit menu.
8. Select Column and then select the <OK> button.

   The column is deleted.

Next, you want to move the Last Name column to the left. If you specifically select the column, then columns A and B will be interchanged.

9. Highlight a cell in column B.
10. Select the Column command from the Select menu.

    The column is highlighted.
11. Select the Move command from the Edit menu.
12. Move the highlight to column A.
13. Press Enter.

    The two report columns are interchanged.

PRACTICE TIME

1. Edit the Intr Report and Intr Page rows to fix the headings.
2. Change the font to a 12-point font, if available.

3. Change the left margin to 2 inches.
4. Preview the report to make sure it looks all right.
5. Return to the list layout.

If you want customer names listed in alphabetical order by last name, you have to sort the database before printing.

PRACTICE TIME

1. Show all records in the database.
2. Sort the database by last name.
3. Rename Report1 as BUSINESS.

Now you are ready to print the report.

1. Select the report BUSINESS from the View menu.
2. Press [Esc] to get to the report screen.
3. Select the Print... command from the Print menu.
4 Select the <Print> button in the dialog box.

   The report is printed.
5. Press [F10] to return to the list layout.

CHANGING THE DATABASE STRUCTURE

Inserting a Field

While you are looking over your reports and patting yourself on the shoulder for a job well done, it occurs to you that you forgot to include a field. The report needs to include a field named Region because there are different sales representatives for each region. The Pacific Northwest is Region 1. Northern California is Region 2, Southern California is Region 3, and Nevada is Region 5.

Does this mean you have to start all over and create a new database? The answer is no. You can modify the database structure to insert a new field.

1. Select the Form command from the View menu option.

The form layout appears.

2. Position the cursor below the Balance field name in the work area.
3. Enter **Region:**.

   The dialog box appears.
4. Set the width to 1.

The Region field has been added to the database.

5. Return to the list layout.
6. Display all records.

The last field in the database is Region. No data are entered in that field yet.

PRACTICE TIME

1. For each record, enter the appropriate value for the Region field:

   Pacific Northwest is Region 1
   Northern California is Region 2
   Southern California is Region 3
   Nevada is Region 5.

   Hints: The state of Oregon is in the Pacific Northwest. The cities of San Jose and Albany are in northern California. Downey and Los Angeles are in southern California.
2. Save the database as CUSTOMR2.
3. Select and display customers in Region 3.

Deleting a Field

The changes you want to make to a database may require that you delete a field. You will now delete the newly inserted Region field for practice.

1. Highlight any cell in the Region field.
2. Select the Delete command from the Edit menu option.

   A dialog box appears.
3. Select the Field option and then select the <OK> button.

   The Region field is deleted.

QUITTING THE SESSION

This is the end of this lesson. Follow the instructions given in Lesson One to quit. Save the changes to your database file.

SUMMARY OF COMMANDS

Topic or Feature	*Command or Reference*	*Menu*	*Page*
Defining a new report	New Report	View	107
Previewing a report from the report screen	Preview...	Print	111
Changing report margins	Page Setup & Margins...	Print	111
Changing report fonts	Fonts...	Format	112
Changing report column width	Select column, then Column Width...	Format	110
Deleting a report column	Highlight the column, then, Delete Row/Column	Edit	116
Inserting a field in a database	In the form layout, locate the highlight, then enter field name followed by :.		117
Deleting a field from a database	Highlight the field name, Delete	Edit	118

SELF-TEST

1. Reports may contain the following row types: ____________________, ________________________, ______________________________, and ____________________.
2. Works generates a report when you select the ______________ command from the ______________ menu option.
3. You arrange the order of records for a report from the ______________ (Report/List) screen.

4. To delete a field from a report, you select the field then select the ______________ command from the ______________ menu option.

5. To delete an unwanted summary line from a report, you select the appropriate ______________ (row/column) then delete it.

6. To print only those records which satisfy certain conditions, the Query is performed from the ______________ (Report/List) screen.

7. To preview a report on the screen, you select the ______________ command from the ______________ menu option.

8. When you have several reports attached to a database file, you can name the reports by selecting the ______________ command from the ______________ menu option.

9. If a report is too wide to fit on one page, two options you have to make it fit are ____ and ______________________________.

10. To insert or delete a field from the database, you can use the ______________ (List/Form/Report) screen.

LESSON ELEVEN

Integrated Tools: Moving Information Between Applications

OBJECTIVES

In this lesson you will learn how to:

- Transfer information among the word processor, spreadsheet, and database applications.

STARTING OFF

Start your computer and enter the Works program so that the initial screen is displayed. Insert your data disk into a disk drive.

Note that before you begin this lesson, you should complete the previous 10 lessons and be sure that you understand how to use the Works word processing, spreadsheet, and database applications. This lesson explains the various steps involved in transferring data between applications.

MOVING INFORMATION FROM SPREADSHEET TO WORD PROCESSING

It is possible for information to be transferred from a spreadsheet into a word processing document. To do so, first you will create a spreadsheet file for data-transfer purposes. Then you will write a word processing document that will be used to receive information from the spreadsheet.

1. Create the spreadsheet file shown on page 122:

	A	B	C	D	E	F
1			SALARY DATA			
2						
3	NAME	NAME			NUM	
4	LAST	FIRST	SEX	DEPT	YEARS	SALARY
5	Barth	Bill	M	Mkt	25	45000
6	Billings	Sandy	F	Acct	30	32000
7	Cole	Ron	M	Sales	10	28000
8	Cotman	Sharon	F	Acct	7	49000
9	Harry	Daria	F	Sales	26	38000
10	Hart	Ed	M	Mkt	4	52000
11	Holloway	Cathy	F	Mkt	7	43595
12	Humphreys	Pat	F	Acct	15	23450
13	Manske	Ken	M	Sales	17	30400
14	McNerney	Charles	M	Mkt	8	42900
15	Myers	Bill	M	Sales	13	37400
16	Nau	Bob	M	Mkt	7	43595
17	Sachs	Arline	F	Mkt	8	42900
18	Thomas	Margaret	F	Sales	11	47000
19	Wiggs	Laura	F	Acct	23	52700
20	Wilkinson	Stan	M	Sales	20	63000

2. Adjust column widths, change the display format for the row headings, and change the font as appropriate.

3. Save the spreadsheet as file SS11 on your data disk.

   Your spreadsheet should be similar to the one shown in Figure 11-1.

Figure 11-1

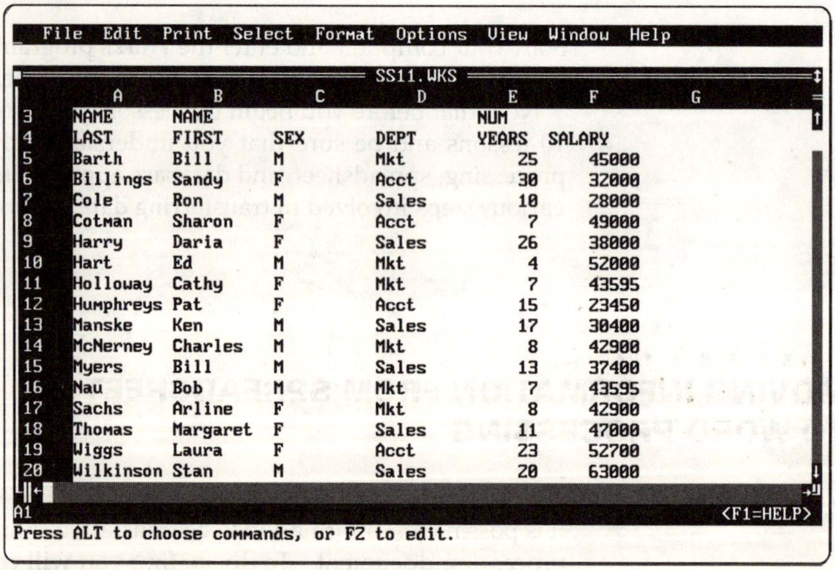

File Edit Print Select Format Options View Window Help

SS11.WKS

	A	B	C	D	E	F	G
3	NAME	NAME			NUM		
4	LAST	FIRST	SEX	DEPT	YEARS	SALARY	
5	Barth	Bill	M	Mkt	25	45000	
6	Billings	Sandy	F	Acct	30	32000	
7	Cole	Ron	M	Sales	10	28000	
8	Cotman	Sharon	F	Acct	7	49000	
9	Harry	Daria	F	Sales	26	38000	
10	Hart	Ed	M	Mkt	4	52000	
11	Holloway	Cathy	F	Mkt	7	43595	
12	Humphreys	Pat	F	Acct	15	23450	
13	Manske	Ken	M	Sales	17	30400	
14	McNerney	Charles	M	Mkt	8	42900	
15	Myers	Bill	M	Sales	13	37400	
16	Nau	Bob	M	Mkt	7	43595	
17	Sachs	Arline	F	Mkt	8	42900	
18	Thomas	Margaret	F	Sales	11	47000	
19	Wiggs	Laura	F	Acct	23	52700	
20	Wilkinson	Stan	M	Sales	20	63000	

A1 <F1=HELP>

Press ALT to choose commands, or F2 to edit.

4. Create a new word processor file and enter the following document, which is incomplete:

MEMORANDUM

DATE: **November 21, 1991**

TO: **Ed Ritenhouse**

FROM: **Marilyn St. Clair**

SUBJECT: **Updated Salary Data**

The following is the salary data for the Marketing, Accounting, and Sales Departments of the company.

5. Press [Enter] to leave a blank line.
6. Use the Save As... command to save the document as file WP11 on your data disk.
7. Switch to the spreadsheet document SS11 using the Window menu option.
8. Select the Copy command from the Edit menu to copy the block A1:F20.
9. Switch back to the word processing document WP11.
10. Press [Enter].

    The spreadsheet information as it appeared on the screen is copied into the word processing document.

11. Finish the letter.

    Would you please verify the data and inform me of any discrepancies with your records?

NOTE: You may have to change the font size of the text just entered.

12. Print the letter. It should look similar to the screen shown in Figure 11-2.

Figure 11-2

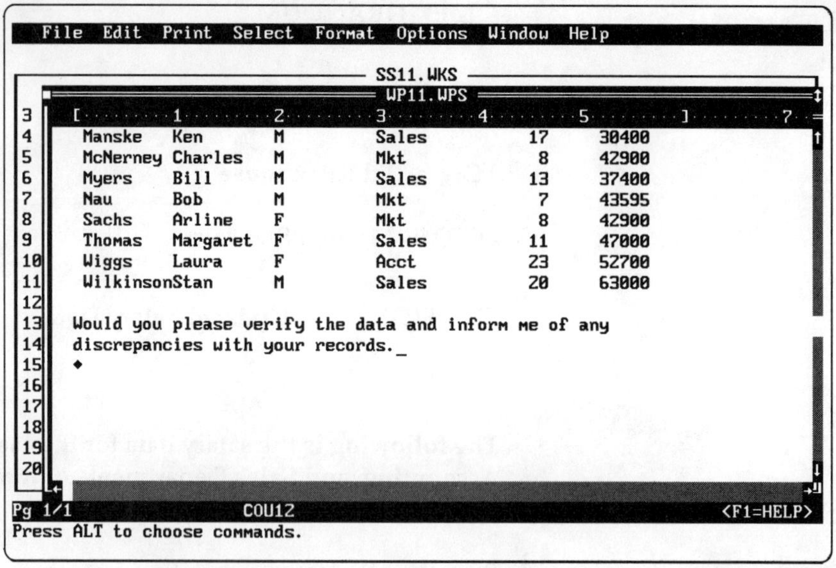

13. Close the word processing file, saving the changes.

MOVING INFORMATION FROM SPREADSHEET TO DATABASE

Next, you will transfer information from a spreadsheet to a database application. You may recall that the spreadsheet display and the list display for database are very similar. Each row of the spreadsheet is considered a record of the database, and each column is a field. That is precisely how the information is transferred between applications. Each row is transferred as a record in the database file, and each column is a field within the record.

First, you need to create a database whose structure corresponds to the format of the spreadsheet file. You can then transfer the information. You will use the spreadsheet SS11 created in the previous section.

1. Create a new database file.
2. Define the following six fields:

LAST NAME:

FIRST NAME:

SEX:

DEPT:

YEARS:

SALARY:

3. Define the format of the last two fields as Fixed with 0 decimal points.

Now that you have a database file defined with the same structure as the spreadsheet file, you can transfer the data.

When you copy information from a spreadsheet to a database, you copy only the data, not the headings and other descriptive information. In the spreadsheet, rows 1 through 4 contain descriptive information, not the actual data. Hence you need to copy information on rows 5 through 20, columns A through F.

1. Switch to the spreadsheet SS11.
2. Select the block A5:F20.
3. Select the Copy command from the Edit menu option.
4. Switch back to the database you just defined.
5. Make sure you are in the list layout.
6. Select the blank cell in the LAST NAME field.
7. Press Enter.

   The information is transferred to the database, as shown in Figure 11-3.

Figure 11-3

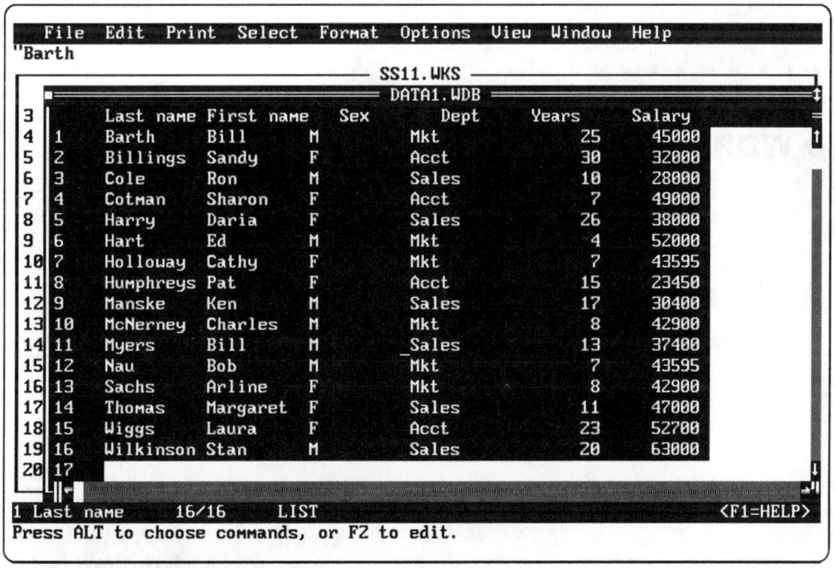

That was easy, wasn't it?

8. Save the database file as DB11 on your data disk.

MOVING INFORMATION FROM DATABASE TO SPREADSHEET

Moving information from a database file to a spreadsheet is just as simple. Information in a database record is transferred into a row in the spreadsheet, with the content of each field transferred into a column of the spreadsheet.

1. Make sure that your database file DB11 is active.
2. Highlight all the fields in all 16 records.

   The entire file is selected.
3. Select the Copy command from the Edit menu option.

   The message line instructs you to select a new location and press Enter.
4. Create a new Spreadsheet file.
5. Select cell A1.
6. Press Enter.

   The database information is copied into the spreadsheet file.

MOVING INFORMATION FROM DATABASE TO WORD PROCESSING

Moving information from a database into a word processing document is similar to moving information from a spreadsheet.

1. Create a new word processing document.
2. Type the following incomplete document:

June 25, 1992
Carol Noonkester
Equal Employment Opportunities Board
P.O. Box 10110
San Francisco, CA 95926

Dear Ms. Noonkester:

The report on company salaries for the Sales Department is as follows:

3. Switch to the database file DB11.
4. Make a query to display only those records for Sales.
5. Return to the list layout.
6. Select all the displayed data.
7. Select the Copy command from the Edit menu option.
8. Select the word processing file from the Window menu option.
9. Position the cursor at the bottom of the document.
10. Press [Enter] to complete the transfer.

    The document looks similar to the one shown in Figure 11-4.

Figure 11-4

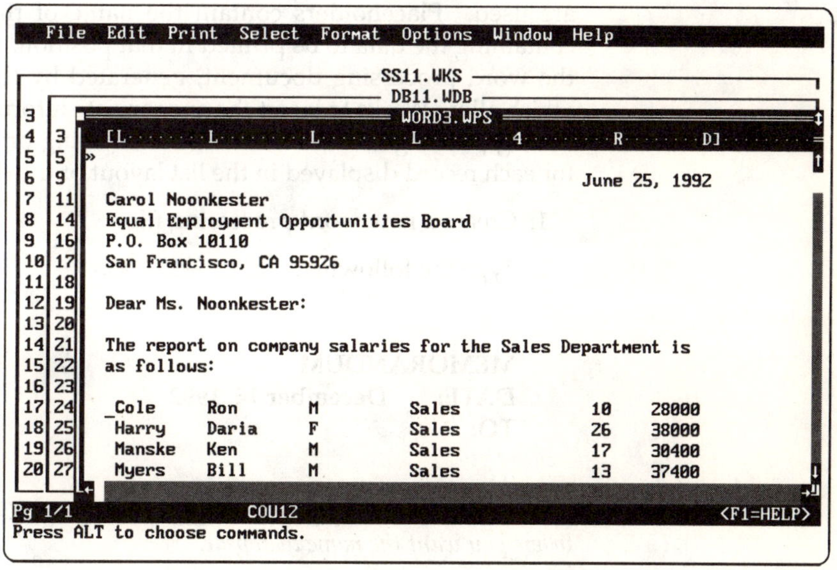

11. You may have to adjust tabs to align the fields.
12. Insert two blank lines beneath the database information.
13. Continue the document with the following text:

    If you have any questions, please contact me.

Sincerely yours,

Marilyn St. Clair

14. Save the word processing document on your data disk as DB2WP.

PRINTING FORM LETTERS USING DATABASE INFORMATION

At times you may need to send the same memo to several people with different addresses, all of which are in a database file. That is when the merge feature—merging information on a database with a word processing document—becomes very useful.

You will use the database file DB11 and insert name, number of years, and salary into a word processing document. To indicate where information from a database is to be inserted into the word processing document, **placeholders** are used. Placeholders contain the name of the database and the field containing the data to be printed in that position. They are internal codes in the word processing document, generated by the Insert Field command, which allow Works to insert the appropriate information from a database file during printing. When form letters are being printed, one letter is printed for each record displayed in the list layout of the database file.

1. Create a new word processing file.
2. Type the following:

MEMORANDUM
DATE: December 14, 1992
TO:

NOTE: Make sure that you press Tab *after typing* ***TO:****, so that the cursor is placed where you want the name to appear.*

Now you are ready to enter the name of the database file.

3. Select the Insert Field... command from the Edit menu option.

   A dialog box appears.

4. Highlight DB11 in the Databases box.

   The fields in DB11 appear in the Fields box.

5. Highlight FIRST NAME and then select the <OK> button.

   The placeholder for the first name field appears on the screen.

6. Press [Spacebar] once to insert a blank space.

7. Use the Insert Field... command to add the LAST NAME placeholder in the document.

8. Continue with the memo, inserting the appropriate placeholder where indicated.

   FROM: Marilyn St. Clair

   SUBJECT: Report to Equal Employment Opportunities Board

   We were recently asked to report your current salary and the number of years you've worked for the company to the Equal Employment Opportunities Board. The following information was supplied.

   Salary: «SALARY»

   Number of Years: «YEARS»

   If you have any questions, please contact me.

   The screen should look similar to Figure 11-5.

9. Save the document as file MERGE11 on your data disk.

Since you reported salary for people in the Sales Department, you must select only those records from the database file before printing.

10. Switch to the database file DB11.

    Make sure that the record selection condition, DEPT=Sales, which you set earlier, is still in effect.

11. Switch back to MERGE11.

12. Select the Print Form Letters... command from the Print menu option.

    A dialog box appears. Make sure that the database file DB11 is selected.

13. Select the <OK> button.

    Another dialog box appears.

Figure 11-5

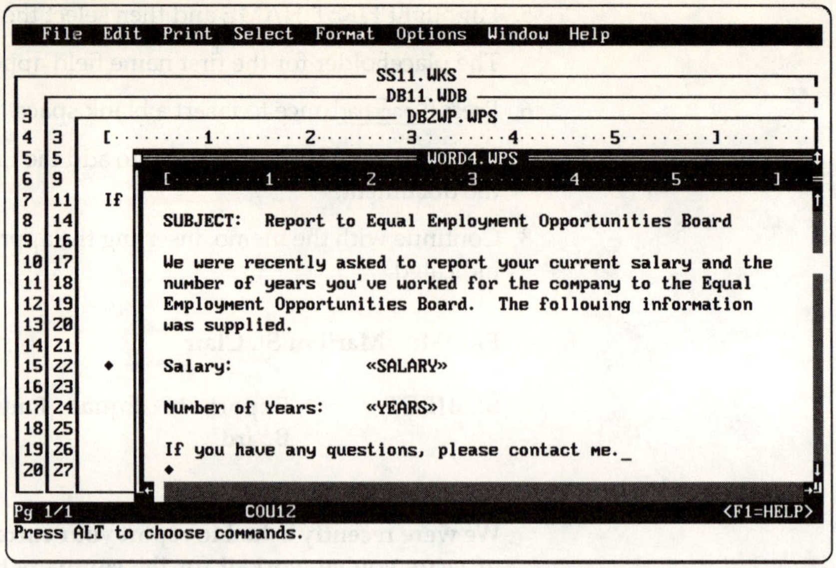

14. Select the <Print> button.

    One memo is printed for each person in the Sales Department.

QUITTING THE SESSION

This is the end of this lesson. Quit the session as described in Lesson One. You may save any changes to the files.

■ *SUMMARY OF COMMANDS*

Topic or Feature	*Command or Reference*	*Menu*	*Page*
Selecting the entire database or spreadsheet	Highlight the fields and records		126
Copying from one application to another	Select the part to be transferred, then copy application name; position cursor, then press Enter	Edit Window	121

Inserting placeholder in word processing document	Position cursor, then Insert Field...	Edit	128
Printing form letters	Print Form Letters...	Print	128

■ *SELF-TEST*

1. When you select spreadsheet rows to transfer information into a database file, you do not want to include ______________.
2. A database file that is to receive information from a spreadsheet must be defined with ______________(fields/records) that correspond to the columns of the spreadsheet.
3. When you copy information from a database to a spreadsheet, the database field names ______________ (are/are not) automatically transferred.
4. To insert a placeholder in a word processing document, use the ______________ command from the ______________ menu option.
5. Form letters are printed using the ______________ command from the ________________________ menu option.

Self-Test Answers

LESSON 1

1. menu bar
2. Alt
3. moving the mouse cursor to the command and pressing the left mouse button
4. Type the highlighted arrow of the command, or use the up and down arrows to highlight the command and press Enter, or move the mouse cursor to the command and press the button.
5. dialog box
6. Save
7 Save As
8. Open Existing File
9. Close
10. Help

LESSON 2

1. holding down Shift while using the arrow keys to highlight the text, or holding down the mouse button while moving the mouse to highlight the text
2. Select the text to be replaced, then select the Typing Replaces Selection Command from the Option menu.
3. move
4. cannot
5. Print
6. Shift
7. beginning-of-page; end-of-file
8. Copy; Edit
9. scrolls up

LESSON 3

1. Page Setup & Margins; Print
2. [;]
3. Indents & Spacing; Format
4. a negative value
5. Tabs; Format
6. Window
7. Both left and right edges of line are flush with margins.
8. Ctrl-U
9. Format
10. Copy Special; Edit

LESSON 4

1. select; Copy; Edit
2. Right; Format
3. Left; Center; Right; Decimal
4. Search; Select
5. Match whole word
6. Insert Page Break command; Print

LESSON 5

1. Go To; Select
2. the entry in the selected cell
3. press Enter; press an arrow key
4. quotation mark

5. a digit or =
6. precede text with "
7. Locate the mouse cursor on the desired cell and press the button.
8. +; –; *; /
9. Clear; Edit
10. Print; Print

LESSON 6

1. =SUM(B1,C1:C3)
2. Relative reference gives general directions; absolute reference specifies the address.
3. The cell is not wide enough to display its numeric contents.
4. Use the Column Width command from the Format menu option.
5. Select those columns before using the Column Width command.
6. It copies the value/text/formula in the leftmost column to columns to the right.
7. It is enclosed in parentheses and contains values/formulas that the function uses.
8. Style; Format
9. It automatically overwrites the earlier version on disk.
10. It automatically prints on multiple pages.

LESSON 7

1. Use the All command in the Select menu option.
2. Style; Format
3. Fixed; Format; Decimals
4. Show Formulas; Options
5. are erased
6. Move; Edit
7. Window
8. Make the other spreadsheet active.
9. select; Delete Row/Column; Edit

LESSON 8

1. fields; database file
2. Format
3. still kept in memory
4. Tab
5. colon (:)
6. List
7. Field Size; Format
8. type the new entry
9. Search; Select
10. Print; Print

LESSON 9

1. Sort Records; Select
2. do not
3. Query; View
4. AND
5. =>100&<200
6. Select one or more fields, choose the Move Field command from the Edit menu, locate the cursor where you want the field(s), and then press Enter.
7. before
8. Select the record; use the Move Record command from the Edit menu.
9. Delete Record; Edit
10. Use a query to display those records in a list layout.

LESSON 10

1. Intr Report; Intr Page; Record; Summ Report
2. New Report; View
3. List
4. Delete Field; Edit
5. row
6. List
7. Report1 (report name); View
8. Preview; Print
9. Use a smaller font; change the margins.
10. Form

LESSON 11

1. row headers (titles)
2. fields
3. are not
4. Insert Field; Edit
5. Print Form Letters; Print

Works 2.0 for the PC Command Summary

Following are most of the commonly used commands in word processing, spreadsheet, and database, including some not covered in this book. Commands for charting or communications are not included.

Topic or Feature	*Command or Reference*	*Menu*
Bold characters (SS, DB)	Style...	Format
Bold characters (WP)	Font & Style...	Format
Bold text	Ctrl-B	
Calculator	Calculator...	Options
Canceling print	Esc	
Centering text (WP)	Center	Format
Centering text (SS, DB)	Style... by centering text	Format
Changing column width (SS)	Select columns, then Column Width...	Format
Changing field display order (DB)	Select the field, then Move, then locate new field position and press Enter	Edit
Character style (WP)	Bold, Underline, Italic, Plain Text	Format
Checking Spelling (WP)	Check Spelling...	Options
Closing a file (exit application)	Close	File
Column deletion (SS)	Select columns, then Delete Row/Column	Edit
Column width (SS)	Select columns, then Column Width...	Format
Copying a record (DB)	Copy Record	Edit
Copying a file	File Management...	File
Copying a formula into cells beneath (SS)	Fill Down	Edit
Copying a formula into cells to the right (SS)	Fill Right	Edit

Copying a record (DB)	Select the record to be copied, then Copy Record, then locate new record position and press [Enter]	Edit
Copying data from one application to another	Select the data to be transferred, then Copy Select file, position cursor, then press [Enter]	Edit Window
Copying disks	File Management...	File
Copying paragraph format (WP)	Copy Special...	Edit
Copying text	Select the text and then Copy	Edit
Creating a new directory	File Management...	File
Creating a new file	Create New File...	File
Creating a report (DB)	New Report...	View
Deleting a file	File Management...	File
Deleting a report (DB)	Reports...	View
Deleting a record (DB)	Select the records, then Delete Record/Field	Edit
Deleting columns (SS)	Select columns, then Delete Row/Column	Edit
Deleting text (WP)	Select the text, then press [Delete]	
Displaying all records (DB)	Show All Records	Select
Displaying hidden records (DB)	Switch Hidden Records	Select
Displaying formulas (SS)	Show Formulas	Options
Displaying only records that meet a condition (DB)	Search... Match All records	Select
Double spacing (WP)	Double Space	Format
Editing an entry (SS)	[F2]	
Editing an existing report (DB)	Select report	View
Entering a formula (SS)	Begin entry with '='.	
Entering multiple selection conditions (DB)	Query	View

Erasing contents of a cell (SS,WP)	Clear	Edit
Exit application (close active file)	Close	File
Exiting Works	Exit	File
Field width (DB)	Field Width...	Format
Finding a cell (SS, DB)	Go To...	Select
Finding text	Search...	Select
First line indent (WP)	Indents & Spacing...	Format
Form layout (DB)	Form	View
Formatting a disk	File Management...	File
Formatting a paragraph (WP)	Indents & Spacing...	Format
Formula display (SS)	Show Formulas	Options
Getting on-screen help	Help	Help Index
Hanging Indent (WP)	Ctrl-H	
Help	Help	Help Index
Indenting paragraph (WP)	Indents & Spacing	Format
Inserting a page break	Insert Page Break	Print
Inserting a placeholder in word processing document	Position cursor, then Insert Field...	Edit
Inserting a record (DB)	Select place in file, then Insert Record/Field	Edit
Inserting a row or column (SS)	Select place in file, then Insert Row/Column	Edit
Inserting special characters (WP)	Insert Special...	Edit
Inserting text	Position the cursor where you want text inserted, then type the text	
Italic	Ctrl-I	
Justification (WP)	Left, Center, Right, Justified	Format
Justifying text entries (SS, DB)	Style... Select alignment	Format
Left justification (WP)	Left	Format
Line spacing (WP)	Single Space, Double Space	Format

List layout (DB)	List	View
Margins	Page Setup & Margins...	Print
Moving a record (DB)	Move Record	Edit
Moving between split screen	F6 or mouse	
Moving cursor or cell highlight	Arrow keys, mouse, scroll bars	
Moving data between files	Select data, then Move Select file Position cursor, press Enter	Edit Window
Moving text	Select data to be moved and then Move Position cursor, press Enter	Edit
Moving window	Move	Window
Multiple selection condition (DB)	Query	View
Numeric display format (SS, DB)	General, Fixed..., Currency..., Comma..., Percent..., Exponential..., True/False, Time/Date...	Format
On-screen help	Help	Help Index
Opening an existing file	Open Existing File...	File
Opening second file	Open Existing File...	File
Page break	Insert Page Break	Print
Page numbering	Headers & Footers... Enter &P command in Header or Footer box	Print
Paragraph format copying (WP)	Copy Special...	Edit
Paragraph indentations (WP)	Indents & Spacing...	Format
Performing a query (DB)	F10	
Placeholder insertion in word processing document	Position cursor, then Insert Field...	Edit
Plain text style (WP)	Plain Text	Format
Printing file	Print...	Print
Printing form letters (WP)	Print Form Letters...	Print

Printing page numbers	Headers & Footers... Enter &P command in header or footer box	Print
Querying (DB)	F10	
Quitting Works	Exit	File
Renaming a file	File Management...	File
Replacing selected text (WP)	Typing Replaces Selection	Options
Replacing all occurrences of text (WP)	Replace...	Select
Right justification (WP)	Right	Format
Ruler display/hide (WP)	Ruler	Options
Saving a file (with new name)	Save As...	File
Saving a file (same name)	Save	File
Searching for text	Search...	Select
Selecting cells (SS)	Position cursor at upper left corner of block; highlight the block and press Enter.	
Selecting columns (SS)	Column	Select
Selecting entire document	All	Select
Selecting fields (DB)	Field	Select
Selecting records (DB)	Record	Select
Selecting rows (SS)	Row	Select
Selecting text or data	*Mouse:* Hold down button while highlighting text or data. *Keyboard:* Hold down Shift while using arrow keys to highlight the text or data.	
Selection conditions (DB)	Query	View
Setting character style (WP)	Bold, Underline, Plain Text	Format
Setting display format of numbers (SS, DB)	General, Fixed..., Currency..., Comma..., Percent..., Exponential..., True/False, Time/Date...	Format
Setting justification (WP)	Left, Center, Justified	Format

Setting line spacing (WP)	Single Space, Double Space	Format
Setting margins	Page Setup & Margins...	Print
Setting paragraph indentations (WP)	Indents & Spacing...	Format
Setting tab stops (WP)	Tabs... Select position, then set alignment to Left, Right, Center, or Decimal	Format
Setting window size	Size	Window
Show ruler (WP)	Ruler	Options
Single spacing (WP)	Single Space	Format
Sorting (SS, DB)	Sort Records...	Select
Spelling checker (WP)	Check Spelling...	Options
Split screen	Split	Window
Switching between open files	Select file	Window
Tab stops (WP)	Tabs...	Format
Thesaurus (WP)	Thesaurus	Options
Underlining text	Ctrl-U	
Undoing last command (WP)	Undo	Edit
Viewing list layout (DB)	List	View
Viewing form layout (DB)	Form	View
Width of columns (SS)	Select columns, then Column Width...	Format
Width of field (DB)	Select field, then Field Width...	Format
Window maximum size	Maximize	Window
Window move	Move	Window
Window size	Size	Window

Index

E

F

G

H

I

J

Q

R

S

T

U

V

W

2